PICTURE BOOKS FOR GIFTED PROGRAMS

by Nancy Polette

The Scarecrow Press, Inc.
Metuchen, N.J., & London
1981

Library of Congress Cataloging in Publication Data

Polette, Nancy.
   Picture books for gifted programs.

   Bibliography: p.
   Includes index.
   1. Gifted children--Education.   2. Picture-
books for children--Educational aspects.
I. Title.
LC3993.2.P64   371.95'3   81-9113
ISBN 0-8108-1461-7   AACR2

CONTENTS

ACKNOWLEDGMENTS

The author is indebted to the following persons who have generously shared their work for inclusion in this text:

Diane Greene for her unit on Humor and Critical Thinking Skills

Jean Engelage for her unit on The Books of Marcia Brown

Joyce Juntune, Executive Director of The National Association for Gifted Children, for her summaries of critical thinking skills and additions to the bibliographies

Evelyn Kasch and Patricia Langford for their unit on The Books of Jean Merrill

Harriet Lippert for her unit on The Books of Daniel Manus Pinkwater

Charlotte Lohrman for her unit on The Books of Jean George

Clarice Marshall for her contributions to the chapter on Jean Piaget and for her additional reviews

Paula Sharp for her unit on Thinking Skills and Fantasy

Dr. Roger Taylor for his Bibliography of Books for Gifted Children and their Teachers

Esther Franklin for the Taxonomy of Visual Communication Skills

INTRODUCTION

In our current emphasis on the basics in American education we are in danger of dimming permanently the light of inquiry and curiosity which shines from the eyes of our brightest children. When competency testing of basic skills takes precedence over the development of productive and critical thinking, the resulting conformity of instruction stifles all but the most persistently searching young minds. It is not surprising, therefore, that the drop-out rate among those secondary school students identified as gifted is high.

Fortunately, Public Law 94-142, which mandates programs for children with special needs, has brought to the attention of parents and educators alike the special needs of the gifted child. Throughout the country educators are beginning to recognize these needs and are attempting to identify unusually gifted and/or talented children and to provide programs and services to meet their needs.

In emerging programs for the gifted, stress on the basic skills is still present, but many of these programs have taken alternative approaches to the skills and in addition to the basics have placed a high priority on the development of critical and productive thinking skills, inductive and deductive reasoning and the development of higher-level communication skills. Early childhood programs for the gifted are examining closely materials and strategies for promoting early cognitive development. Upper elementary and secondary programs are seeking and using resources outside the school setting to provide unique experiences to meet specific needs. Numerous retraining programs and conferences on gifted education have become available to the nation's teachers and many are availing themselves of these in-service opportunities.

While many of these programs for the gifted are in their infancy, a hopeful pattern is emerging. Based on the research of Renzulli, Torrance, Terman, Parnes, Taba, Moffat, Suchman, and many others, these programs for the gifted are stressing fluency and flexibility of thought and originality of responses. In addition, content-oriented subject matter has been replaced with product-oriented activities centered around the critical thinking skills of planning, forecasting, problem solving and decision-making.

This rethinking and restructuring of priorities for gifted education has in turn caused many educational publishers to scramble for materials to toss on the gifted bandwagon. Yet few schools which contain ample picture book collections need look further for imaginative materials to stimulate intellectual skills and creative thought. Children of today are privileged indeed that so many of the most talented and creative thinkers in the picture book world are speaking to them.

Fortunately, in the search for divergent approaches to gifted education the true giftedness of many picture book authors and illustrators has been re-discovered, the myth that the picture book is intended only for the very young has been dispelled and the talent and creative genius which combine to make the picture book more than a simple story have been recognized.

Picture books embody every productive and critical thinking skill to a greater or lesser degree. Cognitive development in early childhood is enhanced by Robert Kraus's The Little Giant (reversibility), Aardema's Who's in Rabbit's House (conservation), Kraus's Milton the Early Riser (seriation), and Spier's Crash Bang Boom and Gobble Growl and Grunt (classification).

Productive thinking is evident in Hoberman's A House Is a House for Me (fluency and flexibility), Anno's Magical Midnight Circus (originality), and the Ahlbergs' Little Worm Book (elaboration).

Countless picture books can be successfully used in stimulating the processes of planning (Boedecker's Mushroom Center Disaster requires the replanning of an entire village); forecasting (what will Grimm's Bearskinner do to regain his soul?); problem solving (how can a small dog be rescued in Van Allsburg's Garden of Abdul Gasazi?), and decision-making (should one take the priceless stone or not in Kennedy's Lost Kingdom of Karnica?).

The choices are endless and the age level at which they are used can extend through the junior high school, for true appreciation of the creative minds and talents involved in the production of a fine picture book can come only as the child achieves a more mature viewpoint.

Finally, if the critical and creative thinking processes embodied in the successful picture book are not sufficient in themselves, there is still the matter of language. That found in the finest picture books is by no means simple and language development should have the highest priority in all educational programs today. For language is the basic tool of thought! It is this reason alone that accounts for book burning in totalitarian societies: when language is simplified, thought becomes simple as well.

Read aloud passages from beautifully illustrated versions of Hans Christian Andersen tales, Rudyard Kipling's Just So Stories or many of Beatrix Potter's tiny volumes. Each has a richness of language seldom heard today and it delights the ear of the three-year-old and the thirteen-year-old alike. It is impossible to read these challenging and entertaining books without opening new worlds of thought and pleasure for children.

When words are confronted in imaginative settings with all their subtleties implied, the child's means of communication and ability to handle ideas are both deepened. The child who is deprived of the richness of language is deprived of more than words, for language is the key to all of life, to all ideas and to all thinking.

The sections which follow describe in some detail picture books which are especially suitable for use in gifted programs. While it is difficult to place a fine picture book within a specific category, an attempt has been made to classify each title within an area where it might prove most useful in developing thinking processes, language development and visual literacy. Categories selected are:

    a.   Books to enhance cognitive development in early childhood

    b.   Books to promote visual literacy

    c.   Books to stimulate language development

    d.   Books to promote productive thinking (fluency, flexibility, originality, elaboration, evaluation)

    e.   Books to stimulate critical thinking (planning, forecasting, problem solving, decision-making).

Each section contains a description of the particular thinking skill area to be developed, followed by an annotated bibliography of titles especially useful in that area.

Part Two of Picture Books for Gifted Programs presents specific strategies for developing the intellectual processes necessary for critical reading, effective communication and original expression. Beginning with units developed around the use of the picture book, Part Two also introduces similar techniques which can be used with titles which have an increasing amount of text, including several junior novels.

It is hoped that Picture Books for Gifted Programs will provide the librarian or teacher with new perspectives on selecting and using picture books with children and with basic strategies for developing critical and productive thinking skills with children at all levels using a variety of fine books.

PART ONE

PICTURE BOOKS FOR THE GIFTED:
NEW PERSPECTIVES IN SELECTION

CHAPTER 1

THE PICTURE BOOK AND PIAGET'S
THEORY OF COGNITIVE DEVELOPMENT

Perhaps more than any single person, Jean Piaget ranks as the giant of contemporary research into the way children think. His demonstrations that learning in young children is creative, developmental and an essential part of living and growing have profound implications both for the curriculum of elementary education and the methods of presenting that curriculum.

The development of a child's mind to its greatest potential is an awesome responsibility for those who have chosen a profession that touches young lives. Yet there is no greater satisfaction than to have helped a child discover his or her feelings, new ways of thinking and, ultimately, new worlds.

Piaget contends that knowledge is neither absorbed passively from the environment nor pre-formed in the child's mind. Nor will it automatically emerge as the child matures. Knowledge is being constructed through interaction between the child's mental structures, experiences and environment. However, maturation, physical growth, and social interaction cannot alone account for intellectual development. Piaget's observations of children revealed patterns in their responses which he determined were reflections of their level of reasoning. The intellectual growth of the child emerges as a result of building on experiences that either fit into the child's level of understanding or are added to what has been acquired. According to Piaget, "the child is the mainspring to his own development."

Intellectual development is the process of restructuring knowledge. An intrusion on the understood way of thinking brings about conflict. The child compensates for his intrusion and seeks to solve the conflict through his or her own intellectual activity, arriving then at a new stage of thinking

3

that generates new understanding and satisfaction. This balance between stability and change is equilibration.

Two other processes are equally important in cognitive development. Assimilation is the process by which the individual integrates new perceptual matter into existing concepts. Intellectual growth takes place when the individual modifies and enriches structures through change. Accommodation occurs when new concepts are added to the framework of knowledge.

An understanding of these processes is essential if teachers are to provide children with opportunities to explore to the fullest the range of thought at a given stage and to build the strongest possible foundation for succeeding stages. When we push children too far beyond their level of understanding we invite failure and inhibit their intellectual development. Yet we must always seek to take the child slightly beyond his or her current level of understanding.

Our goal, as teachers, should be to seek to enrich the environment in such a manner that the child will enjoy learning as intellectual skills are developed. Children's literature provides an abundance of enrichment for the developing mind of the child. The literary experiences we provide can begin early in the formative years and will last a lifetime. Good literature, carefully chosen, can enhance intellectual growth.

Granted, intellectual growth will take place with or without the assistance of good books, but we can greatly improve the quality and quantity of the concepts the child acquires and of the thinking processes he or she employs by exposure to books that will broaden and enhance each area of growth. Each person is the product of the experiences of the formative years. Fine picture books can be among the most meaningful and lasting of all those experiences.

Only by understanding how a child reasons at each stage of his or her growth can we select those literary experiences which are most appropriate, not only for the child's current level of understanding but to help the child reach beyond the range of current reasoning powers to the possibilities that lay ahead.

Piaget defines four basic periods in the cognitive development of an individual. The first stage is the sensori-motor period (0-24 months), in which the development proceeds from reflex activity to a sensorimotor solution to problems. The pre-operational stage (2-7 years) proceeds from the sensorimotor representation to a pre-logical thought pattern to solve problems. For example, during this period the child reasons through his or her observations. If a thing moves it is alive; therefore, cars are alive.

The third period of development (ages 7-11) is that of concrete operations, where the child develops the ability to apply logical solutions. In the fourth period, the period of formal operations, the child moves from logical solutions to concrete problems to all classes of problems including the abstract. In this period the child is finally able to think about thinking!

One of the most crucial stages is the transition between the pre-operational and concrete-operational periods. It is between the ages of four and seven that the child discovers four basic thinking processes which are essential to the acquisition of reading, problem solving, and mathematical skills. These are the thought processes of conservation, reversibility, classification and seriation.

Conservation is the conceptualization that the amount or quantity of matter stays the same regardless of changes in shape or position. The child, for example, who recognizes that Wriggles (from Wriggles, The Little Wishing Pig by Pauline Watson, Seabury, 1979) is still the same pig even though he has acquired the legs of a crane, a tail like a kite and other strange appendages, has achieved a high level of conservation.

Reversibility implies that if thought is reversible, it can follow the line of reasoning back to where it started. Bill Martin Jr.'s Spoiled Tomatoes (Bowmar, n.d.) is a gentle challenge to reversibility in thought, as are Arnold Lobel's A Treeful of Pigs (Greenwillow, 1979) and Judi Barrett's Animals Should Definitely Not Act Like People (Atheneum, 1980). Only when the child is able to follow a line of reasoning back to where it started can he or she successfully embark on problem solving.

Classification logically classifies objects and events, recognizing both their common elements and their differences. There are many fine picture books based on this thinking skill. Peter Spier's book, People (Doubleday, 1980) is filled with fascinating small color sketches which show the diverse forms our common humanity takes. Tana Hoban's Is It Red? Is It Yellow? Is It Blue? (Greenwillow, 1979) classifies objects not only by color but by size, shape and design.

The fourth thinking process to be developed in these early years is seriation, the mental ability to arrange elements according to increasing or decreasing size. It is the ability mentally to order events in a series. This concept can be introduced at very early ages with such books as Mildred Hobzek's We Came A Marching One Two Three (Four Winds, 1978), Anita Lobel's The Pancake (Greenwillow, 1979), Donald Crews' Freight Train (Greenwillow, 1979), or even through such simple games and books as Diane Zuromskis' The Farmer in the Dell (Little-Brown, 1979).

Piaget reminds us that every experience is unique and that every experience the child has will affect the intellect. His theory of cognitive development provides a logical base for the selection of books to share with children. In our quest for specific titles we must not, however, ignore recognized standards for judging a fine picture book, for our choice must center upon finding the very best literature to share.

In selecting titles to be reviewed in this section the four basic thinking tasks outlined above were of primary consideration. However, other basic considerations were the following:

a. Is the book good literature?

b. Does it make a significant contribution to the child's vision, wisdom, enjoyment or appreciation of beauty?

c. Does the book broaden the child's horizons, stimulate new understanding and build on previously formed concepts?

d. Does the book have true child appeal?

e. Does it deal with one or more of the tasks of cognitive development?--i. e., conservation, classification, seriation, reversibility?

Picture books can open up the world of literature to the receptive, formative mind of the child while teaching him or her to live life to the fullest. Good books do shape young minds and our challenge is to direct wisely by providing those books which will build on each experience. The debate continues as to whether the cognitive tasks of early childhood can be accelerated, yet no controlled studies have been done on the effect of carefully chosen children's books in nurturing this development. A representative group of books for this purpose follows. The challenge lies ahead for every teacher or librarian who works with gifted children to examine newer titles and to reexamine older books to find others of equal challenge.

Anno, Mitsumasa. Anno's Counting Book. Illus. by the
    author. Thomas Y. Crowell Co., 1975.
       This appealing introduction to numerals requires the reader to search for the objects to match the numerals on each page. The book begins with a winter scene showing a snow covered field and a bare sky. As the numbers increase the objects increase, challenging the mind to find and classify the objects.
       As the numerals grow the seasons also change, until the reader has experienced the full cycle of the seasons. Each page is colorful and challenging and requires an attentive reader.
       The author-illustrator presents a wide variety of objects which give meaning to the numerals. Anno provides the reader an enjoyable and useful lesson in one-to-one correspondence, matching and comparing. Without using words he introduces our number system by showing mathematical relationships in nature. This is an excellent title for reinforcing both seriation and classification.

Balian, Lorna. The Aminal. Abingdon, 1972.
       "Patrick was having a picnic all by himself when he saw it." Feeling it much better to picnic with a friend, Patrick captures the "Aminal." He makes it a bed in his lunch sack and heads for home. Patrick meets Molly on the way home and describes his "Aminal" but does not show it to Molly. The tale of this "Aminal" travels from Molly to Calvin to Freddie to Cookie to Geraldine. Each time the "Aminal" is described, it becomes more horrifying. The friends become alarmed that Patrick is in great danger and is too small to know any better. They must save their friend! By the time they find Patrick, the "Aminal" has disappeared. After a long search, Patrick discovers "it" under the porch. To the reader's and other children's amazement "The Aminal" is only a little green turtle.

While this delightful tale requires the child to reverse and revise thinking patterns, it is also a humorous example of Piaget's theory of assimilation. Each child in the story attempts to assimilate the verbal descriptions of the "Aminal" into his or her own store of knowledge. When this doesn't work, the child develops a new concept to reach accommodation.

Balian, Lorna. The Humbug Witch. Abingdon, 1970.

Is the witch a girl or is the girl a witch? The "Humbug Witch" is a very little witch, but a very ferocious ugly witch. She has all the traits of your average witch: the nose, teeth, stringy hair, hat, black shoes, etc. --right down to the broom and her black cat, Fred. This is all very well and good except that every time this little witch tries to do anything witchy, it never turns out witchy. No matter how hard she tries her broom will not go, her magic words accomplish

nothing, even her Magic Potion (made from an unbelievably good recipe) only makes Fred sick. Finally, the "Humbug Witch" decides to give up. She takes off all her witchy attire including her stringy red hair and her mask with its ugly long nose and teeth. What a SURPRISE--under all that is a darling little girl who goes to bed.   (Conservation)

Barrett, Judi. Animals Should Definitely Not Act Like
     People. Illus. by Ron Barrett. Atheneum, 1980.
        Animals are really quite successful at being just what they are: animals. They have their own lifestyle, and they manage very well at it, all things considered. If they did try to act like people the results would be preposterous, outrageous, silly, troublesome, and even dreadfully dull. To illustrate that this is true, Judi and Ron Barrett examine the plight of the hippo trying to take a bath, the ostrich playing outfield on a baseball team, a ladybug trying to get her groceries home, and a turtle trying to manage an umbrella in a

thunderstorm. Ridiculous! But then, the main reason why
animals should definitely not act like people is that we wouldn't
like it--for reasons that are all too obvious when it is you
looking out through the zoo bars at the animals who have come
to watch what you do. A delightful exercise in reversibility
of thought!

Bonsall, Crosby. Who's Afraid of the Dark? Illus. by the
    author. Greenwillow, 1980.
       A small boy has a dog named Stella who he feels must
have a serious problem. He thinks she is afraid of the dark.
Stella isn't aware of this as she immediately drops off to
sleep on the rug beside the boy's bed. Her master imagines
that Stella sees scary things and shivers in fear. She hears
steps on the roof but he tries to reassure her by telling her
it must be raindrops. The boy hides under the covers and
experiences all the fears he thinks Stella feels, while the dog
sleeps soundly on the rug by the bed.
       A friend shows the boy how to help Stella get over
being afraid of the dark. He must hug her and hold her to
drive away her fears. The next night when the boy thinks
Stella is beginning to shiver and see scary things and hear
steps on the roof, he wakes up and pulls her into his bed.
He hugs and holds her. It works! Stella is no longer afraid
of the dark. In fact, no one in the room is afraid of the dark
anymore and both Stella and the boy are soon sound asleep.
       The story challenges the young reader or listener to
reverse thinking. The text and the illustrations contradict
each other and the child who can distinguish the literal from
the implied meaning has achieved the thinking skill of reversibility.

Brown, Marcia. Once a Mouse (Fable from India). Charles
    Scribner's Sons, 1961 (K-2).
       The author-artist has used woodcuts in illustrating this
fable of India. Taking full advantage of her medium, she has
allowed the texture or grain of the wood to show through, adding depth and interesting pattern to her dramatic illustrations. This Caldecott winner concerns a hermit who pondered
big and little. A mouse was nearly caught by a crow and
then a cat. Using magic, the hermit changed the mouse into
a cat, and as it was threatened, into a dog, and then into a
tiger. When the hermit scolded the tiger for being so proud,
the tiger decided to kill the hermit. Alas! He was changed
back to a mouse.

In this real challenge to the child's sense of conservation and reversibility, the tiger's shadow is shaped like the dog of his previous existence and the jungle pattern is shaped like a tiger leaning toward the final mouse form. In order to signify danger, Miss Brown has added red to the pictures. Starting with cool forest green, mustard yellow, and a trace of red, the red builds up to increasing amounts until the climax is reached and the tiger is changed back to a mouse. The last picture is without any reds and shows the hermit is once again "thinking about big--and little...."

(Conservation, Reversibility)

Carle, Eric. Twelve Tales from Aesop. Philomel Books, 1980.

Even the youngest child should be able to identify the structure of a fable if exposed to this form of literature. Certainly, as a step toward achieving conservation, kindergarten and primary children should be helped to see that the animals in the stories are really people in disguise and that each tale contains a piece of good advice--a sort of hidden message from Aesop.

Eric Carle's bright illustrations are filled with details that will enrich the child's enjoyment of the fables while adding an element of wry social commentary for the older child astute enough to catch it. (Conservation)

Charlip, Remy, and Moore, Lilian. Hooray for Me! Illus. by Vera B. Williams. Originally from Parents Magazine Press. Reissued by Four Winds, 1980.

Vera Williams' blurry watercolors make a delectable rainbow out of a row of narrow city houses from which emerge countless children, all celebrating their separate selfhood. The children and their words tumble about engagingly, and in a delightful introduction to classification by relationship, they introduce themselves: "I am my big sister's baby brother." "I am my dog's walker." "I am this book's reader." Young readers should be challenged to classify themselves in as many ways as possible.

Elting, Mary and Folsom, Michael. Q Is for Duck. Illus. by Jack Kent. Houghton Mifflin/Clarion Books, 1980.

"Q is for duck. Why? Because a duck quacks."

In this alphabet guessing game the child's sense of classification is strongly challenged as he or she delights in guessing why A is for zoo (because animals live in the zoo), or "Why E is for whale?" (because whales are enormous). As each alphabet animal is revealed the child will mentally begin a game of association, searching for common elements all beginning with the same letter which are related to the animal. While the book is intended for very young readers, even older students and adults will find a challenge in forming the associations necessary for this alphabet guessing game. (Classification/Analysis)

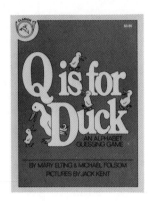

Hill, Donna. Mr. Peeknuff's Tiny People. Illus. by Alan Daniel. Atheneum, 1981.

To Mr. Peeknuff, who lives high on a hill, everyone and everything in the valley below looks small. He thought of Widow Hasty and Farmer Chore and Baker Soone and all the others there as the tiny people. Because he liked the tiny people, on a day when a terrible wind created all kinds of disasters, Mr. Peeknuff hurried down the mountain to help them. Unfortunately (and to the amusement of children who have achieved conservation), he could not find them. There were many big people in trouble but no tiny people. What could have happened to them? Mr. Peeknuff never found out, but this challenging spoof on perspective will delight many young readers or listeners who do know! (Conservation)

Janosch. Hey, Presto! You're A Bear! Illus. by the author. An Atlantic Monthly Press Book. Little Brown, 1977.

Here is magic at its best in Janosch's story of a boy who turns his father into a bear. "Hey, Presto! You're a bear!" The magic works its mischief, and the boy and bear are off on a grand spree. Children will delight in this fantasy of control where roles are reversed through the author's witty and perceptive imagination which is sympathetic to the problems of both children and adults. (Reversibility)

Kahl, Virginia. Whose Cat Is That? Illus. by the author.

Charles Scribner's Sons, 1979.

A small, white, homeless cat wanders into a town and begins an unusual adventure (for a cat). She meets a lady who immediately adopts and names her for her own. The cat's curiosity encourages her to wander on to house after house, and she is fed, adopted and named again by a member of each household. She enjoys a variety of foods and acquires a very long name for one cat.

The small cat happily settles down to being everyone's cat until one day a new law is passed stating that every house must have its own cat. When the inspectors come to check the villagers realize that they must trick the inspectors into believing that every house has a cat. At this point the child's sense of conservation is challenged as the cat goes through many visual changes while being switched from house to house ahead of the inspectors. The clever deceptions of the townspeople in fooling the inspectors provide a hilarious problem-solving situation for the young reader to savor.

(Conservation)

Kalan, Robert. Blue Sea. Illus. by the author. Greenwillow, 1979.

A little fish swims away from big fish; they swim away from bigger fish; and all swim away from the biggest fish. They swim through successively smaller holes until there is only one little fish left in his blue sea. This is a simple introduction to seriation for the youngest, with eye-catching yellow, green, pink and orange fish in a bright blue sea.

(Seriation)

Lionni, Leo. The Greentail Mouse. Illus. by the author. Pantheon, 1973.

This tale, through the device of masks, explores the conservation concept of appearance versus reality. In deciding to have their own Mardi Gras celebration, the field mice don spine-chilling animal masks. As they throw themselves completely into the celebration they begin to lose their original identity and come to believe that they really are the animals they are portraying. When the Greentailed Mouse arrives on the scene he is mistaken for a giant mouse, but manages to convince the revelers that if they take off their masks they will all be themselves again. (Conservation)

Lobel, Arnold. A Treeful of Pigs. Illus. by Anita Lobel. Greenwillow, 1979.

It was the farmer's idea to buy the pigs. "We will look after them together," he promised his wife. But when they got the pigs home, the farmer was too busy sleeping to help--even when the pigs bloomed in the garden like flowers, or hung, like apples, from the tree.

For a while the farmer's wife did all the work, until the day came when she decided to wake her husband up once and for all. And after that, they took care of the pigs together.

Children will enjoy the bright, witty language and the reversal of traditional roles. Some may even be able to help the farmer's wife solve her problem of too many pigs and not enough help. (Reversibility)

Marzollo, Jean. Close Your Eyes. Illus. by Susan Jeffers. Dial Press, 1978.

Jean Marzollo's charming lullaby is beautifully illustrated by Susan Jeffers. The delicate and fanciful pictures actually tell two stories: the child's view of bedtime and her father's version of the event. The menagerie in the illustrations are all in a sleepy mood, while the child is energy in motion until the end. Visual perception is a vital part of this book, which challenges the child's ability to reverse his perceptions in contrasting action and mood of both characters and scenes. (Reversibility)

Mathews, Louise. The Great Take-Away. Illus. by Jeni Bassett. Dodd Mead, 1980.

Subtraction and reversibility are closely related concepts and here is a delightful introduction to both. The hero of the tale is a pig who is a masked thief with a minus sign on his shirt. The young reader meets a subtraction problem each time our pig thief steals from his fellow pigs. The process is reversed when the thief is caught and all the loot hidden in his large black cape is revealed. (Reversibility)

Noble, Trinka Hakes. The Day Jimmy's Boa Ate the Wash. Illus. by Steven Kellogg. Dial Press, 1980.

This story-hour find for the very youngest tells a tale from the end to the beginning! This zany and humorous introduction to reversibility is sure to be a hit with pre-school, kindergarten children. The story begins (ends!) as a little girl arrives home from a class trip to the farm. She answers her mother's question about the day by saying that the trip was rather dull until:

"The cow started crying."

"A cow crying?" asks mother.

"Yeah, you see a haystack fell on her."

"But a haystack doesn't just fall over."

"It does if the farmer crashes into it with his tractor."
And so the story goes back and back to the first incident of
the trip when "Jimmy's boa ate the wash." (Reversibility)

Saunders, Susan. Wale's Tale. Illus. by Marilyn Hirsch.
   The Viking Press, 1980.
      How does one go about changing a donkey into a prince?
This becomes Sara's problem as she meets a talking donkey
on her way to sell vegetables at the market. The donkey
strikes a bargain with her. He will help her sell her vegetables if she will help him become a prince once again.
      Young children will delight in Sara's solution to the
problem, and those capable of reversibility of thought will take
special pleasure in the ending, which requires the child to
back up and take another long look at the entire story! Delightful for reading aloud or alone. (Reversibility)

Worth, Valerie. Curlicues. The Fortunes of Two Pug Dogs.
   Illus. by Natalie Babbitt. Farrar, Straus and Giroux,
   1980.
      Here is a delightful study of contrasts and role re-
versal. In an age of antimacassars and ottomans, fern stands
and tea caddies, parlors and cooks and housemaids, two curly-
tailed pug dogs find themselves purchased by two old ladies,
one plump and kindly, the other thin and severe.
      The thin old lady cares only for her pug's usefulness
as a watchdog, and insists that he be fed nothing but the
meager scraps from her table, while the plump old lady (abet-
ted by her amicable housemaid) treats her own dog to cakes
and chocolates as well as specially prepared dinners--until
her bad-tempered cook rebels. The thin old lady also meets
with an opponent in the person of her downtrodden housekeeper.
The two plots thicken until both households are thrown into a
turmoil, resolved only when the pugs themselves lead the
other characters to a highly satisfactory conclusion.
                                          (Reversibility)

Yolen, Jane. All in the Woodland Early. Illus. by Jane
   Zalben. Collins-World, 1979.
      The alphabet is presented in an appealing manner by

using woodland creatures. Some of the animals are familiar; others are unusual and will be an addition to a child's nature vocabulary. The progression of the alphabet is done in rhyme and rhythm, adding to the charm the woodland creatures naturally have for children. The repetition in verse appeals to young readers while reinforcing classification skills.

The illustrations are artistically done in full color, complementing the verse of the book. An added bonus comes at the end of the book when we find the verse has been put to music. Its esthetic beauty adds to the value of the book as it develops associative thinking skills that will be invaluable to children. (Classification)

Piaget's Theory of Cognitive Development: Some Helpful Resources

Bearley, M., ed. The Teaching of Young Children: Some Applications of Piaget's Learning Theory. New York: Schocken Books, 1976.

Furth, H. G. and Henry Wachs. Thinking Goes to School. New York: Oxford University Press, 1974.

Ginsberg, H. and S. Opper. Piaget's Theory of Intellectual Development. Englewood Cliffs, N. J.: Prentice-Hall, 1969.

Lavatelli, C. S. A Piaget Program. Boston: Center for Media Development, 1970.

Lavatelli, C. S. Piaget's Theory Applied to an Early Childhood Curriculum. Cambridge, Mass.: Center for Media Development, American Science & Engineering, Inc., 1976.

Piaget, J. Behavior and Evolution. New York: Random House, 1976.

Piaget, J. The Language and Thought of the Child. New York: New American Library, 1974.

Piaget, J. Six Psychological Studies. New York: Random House, 1968.

Pulaski, M. S. Understanding Piaget. New York: Harper and Row, 1971.

Sharp, Evelyn. Thinking Is Child's Play. New York: Avon Books, 1969. Paperback.

Sime, M. A Child's Eye View. New York: Harper and Row, 1973.

Singer, Dorothy and Tracey Revenson. A Piaget Primer: How a Child Thinks. New York: International Universities Press, 1978.

CHAPTER 2

VISUAL COMMUNICATION

Reading instruction in the elementary school centers upon the teaching of word attack and comprehension skills. No one would deny the necessity of helping children to acquire these skills, yet they often comprise the total program of reading. Here is where the basic problem lies.

A reader has been defined as one who sustains the reading activity for considerable lengths of time because of the sheer joy found in the reading experience. Whatever the critics say, we are doing an excellent job of teaching reading in the schools today. The literacy rate in the United States is 97 per cent! Yet, we are not creating readers if one accepts the definition above. Only 16 per cent of American adults read one or more books a year!

It would seem then, that a re-definition of the reading process is necessary if the schools are to go beyond the teaching of reading skills toward the goal of developing readers in the fullest sense.

Simply put, reading is the creation of visual images. Lloyd Alexander describes the process in these words:

> Most magical of all, intangible yet durable, are the mental images evoked by literature. Here there is no artifact, no external object of contemplation, no hallucinogen--only language. Words read and spoken----.
>
> (Language Arts, April 1978)

The child whose total concern is the correct pronunciation of each written word sees only a series of unrelated words. A sentence, far from evoking a visual image, is seen as an unrelated series of hurdles to jump in order to be a winner in the reading race.

18

Bill Martin, Jr., in his nationally acclaimed teacher seminars, states the problem another way. "Teachers," he says, "assume that the word is the basic unit of language. This is not true. The sentence is the basic unit of language, for only the sentence can form a complete visual image."

The implications of this re-definition of the reading process are far-reaching for those involved in gifted education.

Among the many criteria used in identifying students for participation in gifted programs are standardized achievement tests. These are tests of basic knowledge and skills and, of necessity, are convergent in nature. They identify, not necessarily the gifted child, but the academically talented. These children are more often than not convergent thinkers and are quite comfortable with the 70 to 80 per cent of the school day that is spent in skills and knowledge areas.

Gifted programs, on the other hand, stress productive and critical thinking and creation of products by the child rather than skills in the knowledge and comprehension areas. In this program, the ability mentally to visualize a scene, a problem, a pattern or a solution is essential.

For example, the child who attempts a creative writing exercise is often attacked by writer's block because of inability to switch from the left (factual, analytical or skills) side of the brain to the right (visual, emotional) side of the brain. Early experiences which help children to visualize detail are therefore essential. If one cannot form mental images of great clarity, then it is impossible to create images through the written word for others.

One of the major tasks of the brain is to filter out from the thousands of visual stimuli, that image most important to the moment. It is possible to see hundreds of images at one time, yet to focus on the one which is of most importance. Attempting to absorb all that we see is an impossible task, but learning to observe more closely and with all of the senses is not only possible but highly desirable.

In an article entitled "Why Children Should Draw: The Surprising Link Between Art and Learning" (Saturday Review, September 3, 1977), Roger M. Williams states:

> If current thinking is correct that the arts come out of the right, or visual side, you are ob-

viously damaging the brain if you don't cultivate that side as well as the analytic side.... Lack of stimulation ... leads to inhibitions in the motor cortex and to inability to think certain kinds of thoughts and feel certain kinds of feelings.

Visual Communication Defined

Visual communication can best be defined by a look at the specific skills involved. Certainly perception and awareness are key components in its development. This includes perception of graphic forms, color, shadings/light contrasts, figures, patterns, and detail. Numerous books highlight these components.

Tana Hoban's classic, Look Again (Macmillan 1971), is an excellent example of a book which will help young children to perceive and to be able to contrast and identify items by size, shape, texture and pattern. In addition, color, shadings and light contrasts form the basis of her more recent book for primary children, Is It Red? Is It Yellow? Is It Blue? (Greenwillow 1978).

Janina Domanska deals directly with perspective as she gives the viewer a dachshund's-eye view of the world through the seasons in her book, Spring Is (Greenwillow 1976).

Beau Gardner in The Turn About, Think About, Look About Book (Lothrop, Lee and Shepard, 1980) challenges the older viewer's sense of perspective, for each of his graphic illustrations can be seen four different ways, depending on the angle of view.

The master of detail, Mitsumasa Anno, provides a wealth of visual experiences for children and adults in his Anno's Medieval World. With a brief poetic text and richly hued and detailed paintings Anno brilliantly evokes the spirit of the time: its culture and beliefs, fears and superstitions, as well as the growing advances in scientific thought and inquiry. Even the most visually literate viewer will need many hours with this and other of Anno's books to savor all that the artist has provided.

Helping younger readers to look more closely is the Ahlbergs' book, Each Peach Pear Plum (Viking, 1979). It invites children to play "I Spy" and find the semi-hidden nursery rhyme characters in each of the appealing water-color illustrations.

The visually literate person understands how messages and moods are communicated through art. He or she is able to interpret action in illustration, react verbally to visual work, can read simple body language and can identify work which communicates specific mood. For the very young child, the wordless picture books of Mercer Mayer are ideal. Ah-Choo (Dial, 1976), Bubble Bubble (Dial, 1967), Hiccup (Dial, 1976) and Oops (Dial, 1977) all lend themselves to oral interpretation of humorous action.

Raymond Briggs brings both action and mood to the viewer in his wordless story of a poignant relationship of a small boy and a snowman in The Snowman (Random, 1979). In describing The Snowman as a visual tour, Hornbook Magazine says: "Again, as in Father Christmas (Coward, 1973), the artist develops narrative, plot and characterization in a sequence of blocks and strips, which at moments of dramatic intensity expand into full-page scenes or double-page spreads. Softly textured pictures in mellow, subdued color add a lyrical quality to the story as it rises and falls to an inevitable end."

As Anno is the master of detail so is Ed Young a master of mood. In White Wave, a haunting tale of a moon goddess and the poor fisherman she befriends, the artist keeps before the viewer the subtle but ever-present image of the wave which draws the reader from one page to the next (White Wave by Diane Wolkstein; Crowell, 1979).

The visually literate person can identify simple symbols and their meaning, can verbalize the meanings of symbols used in place of words and can interpret symbolic relationships and creative meaning from symbols. Ed Young's illustrations in White Wave are excellent examples of symbolic representation as well as an artistic achievement of mood. How many readers will note the similarity in shape of White Wave's hair and the temple spires? For those who do see, few will take that next step toward symbolic awareness unless helped to do so.

A masterful achievement of symbolism for older readers is Children of the Sun by Jan Carew (illustrated by Leo and Diane Dillon; Little, Brown, 1980). The tale weaves together the threads of several universal myths whose protagonists are half-human and half-god, symbolizing numerous elements of nature and of human nature. Symbolism is evident not only in the figures of the story but in the subtle shadings and light sources. In one magnificent illustration a fire glows on the faces of those gathered around it, yet light shines, too, on the face of a woman far removed from the fire. What is the light source? Where does it come from? What does it symbolize?

The reviews which follow are of books specifically chosen to develop one or more aspects of visual communication. The artists and authors who created them are masters at their craft and no age limit for introducing them to children should be set. Categories used in the selection of the titles were:

Perception of Graphic Forms
Perception of color, shading/light contrast
Perception of detail
Interpretation of action and mood
Use and interpretation of symbols.

Preceding the reviews is the Taxonomy of Visual Communication Skills developed by the Library/Media personnel of schools in El Dorado, Placer, Sacramento and Yolo Counties in California under the direction of Esther Franklin. Those selecting books for gifted programs should find it invaluable in defining the skills specifically.

VISUAL COMMUNICATION: A TAXONOMY

Sample Behavioral Objectives: 1. When given two books, 1st grade student can identify which is illustrated with photographs and which with artist-drawn pictures; student also can verbalize in two or three sentences the differences in materials needed for the two different techniques. 2. Given packet of eight photographs, 9th grade student can select three created by Dorothea Lange and verbalize method of identification.

S K I L L S	PRI K-3	INT 4-6	JH 7-9	HS 10-12
Developed by Media/Library Personnel from schools in El Dorado, Placer, Sacramento and Yolo Counties in California. Editor: Esther Franklin.				
I. Demonstrates Awareness and Perception of Graphic Forms				
A. Names items	E-----P	P	P	P
B. Identifies items by size, shape	E-----P	P	P	P
C. Discriminates size (large, small, etc.)	E-----P	P	P	P
D. Communicates about position, e.g., up, over	E-----P	P	P	P
E. Identifies tactile qualities, e.g., hardness, softness	E--------P		P	P
F. Understands how patterns are formed		E--------P	P	P
G. Can verbalize the contrasts in two patterns		E--------P	P	P

VISUAL COMMUNICATION

S K I L L S	PRI K-3	INT 4-6	JH 7-9	HS 10-12
II. Demonstrates Awareness and Perception of Color/Shadings/Light Contrasts				
A. Recognizes primary colors	E-----P	P	P	P
B. Identifies shades as colors	E-------	-------P	P	P
C. Distinguishes light, dark, shadows in illustrations and photos	E-------	-----------	-----------	-P
III. Demonstrates Awareness and Perception of Figures, Human and Others				
A. Names by types, e.g., man, woman	E-----P	P	P	P
B. Recognizes by nationalities	E-------	-------P	P	P
C. Identifies by size	E-------	-------P	P	P
D. Communicates about relationships on page, in picture, on flannel board, etc.	E-------	-------P	P	P
E. Can theorize action by position of figures, e.g., running, fighting, etc.	E-------	-------P	P	P

VISUAL COMMUNICATION

S K I L L S	PRI K-3	INT 4-6	JH 7-9	HS 10-12
IV. Understands Symbols and Their Use				
A. Can identify simple symbol as request for action, e.g., stop sign	E	------P	P	
B. Can verbalize meaning of symbol which replaces series of words	E		------P	P
C. Can interpret creative meaning from symbols, e.g., dove for peace	E			------P
V. Familiar With Vocabulary of Visual Communications				
A. Can cite at least three important words essential to filmmaking, e.g., fade-out		E	------P	P
B. Can recognize at least five terms related to illustrating technique	E	------P	P	P
C. Seeks materials which enhance understanding of Visual Communications	E	------P	P	P
VI. Has Developed Introductory Understanding of Graphic Techniques				P

VISUAL COMMUNICATION

S K I L L S	PRI K-3	INT 4-6	JH 7-9	HS 10-12
A. Can distinguish between photograph and illustration	E------P	P	P	P
B. Can distinguish between major types of illustration, e.g., woodcuts and water colors	E--------------------P			P
C. Can recognize two major types of techniques in illustration	E--------------------P		P	P
D. Can identify at least one artist's work by technique	E--------------------P	P	P	P
VII. Demonstrates Awareness and Perception of Combined Elements of Illustration, Photograph, Painting, Filmstrip, etc.				
A. Can distinguish figures from background	E--------------------P		P	P
B. Can verbalize on perspective (far away, close, etc.)	E--------------------P	P	P	P
C. Can communicate about relationships within work, e.g., the pointed line contrasted to the general spherical elements		E--------------------P	P	P
D. Can comment on design		E--------------------P	P	P

VISUAL COMMUNICATION

S K I L L S	PRI K-3	INT 4-6	JH 7-9	HS 10-12
VIII. Understands How Messages Are Communicated Visually				
A. Can "read" a simple photograph	E-------P	-------P	P	P
B. Can interpret action in illustration	E-------	-------P	-------P	P
C. Can determine sequence in series of pictures	E----P	P	P	P
D. Can identify specific film, etc. which communicates specific message without words	E--------	-------P	P	P
E. Can identify specific photographer whose photographs convey specific message		E--------		-------P
F. Can identify specific illustrator whose illustrations convey specific message	E--------	-------P	P	P
IX. Understands How Moods Are Communicated Visually				
A. Can read simple body language, e.g., displeasure	E--------	-------P	P	P
B. Can react verbally to visual work, e.g., "It made me sad," or "I think it seems spooky."		E--------		-------P

VISUAL COMMUNICATION

S K I L L S	PRI K-3	INT 4-6	JH 7-9	HS 10-12
C. Can identify work which communicates specific mood	E	------P	P	P
D. Can identify an author or photographer whose art communicates mood			E	------P
X. Understands Use of Visual Communications				
A. Able to select illustrations which have brought sustained pleasure, or other emotion	E	------P	P	P
B. Able to name film in which people did actions with which viewer could identify		E		------P
C. Can cite a photograph or collection of photographs which conveyed problems of other people not previously known to viewer		E	------P	P
D. Able to identify a value, e.g., beauty, love, etc., discovered through visual perception		E	------P	P
XI. Demonstrates Appreciation of Visual Communications				
A. Seeks specific works of selected illustrators	E	------P	P	P
B. Wants to study art prints voluntarily and requests to take home		E		------P

VISUAL COMMUNICATION

S K I L L S	PRI K-3	INT 4-6	JH 7-9	HS 10-12
C. Asks for more photographs taken by photographer studied			E-------P	P
D. Requests opportunity to view film or filmstrip repeated number of times	E-------P		P	P
E. Suggests formation of school organization related to visual communications		E------P	P	P
F. Actively participates in organization		E------P	P	P

Ahlberg, Janet and Allan. Each Peach Pear Plum. Viking, 1979.
    This graceful and pleasant book invites children to play 'I Spy' and point out nursery rhyme and story characters who are partly hidden within the illustrations. The pictures contain action and humor and evoke beauty of the English countryside. The clever hiding places of the characters have at times fooled adults looking at the book with children. An excellent book for helping children to look closely.

Anno, Mitsumasa. Anno's Animals. Illus. by the author. William Collins, 1977.
    Anno has hidden a menagerie of animals in a woodsy setting in this wordless book. The book is a delightful challenge in visual awareness.
    The delicate, ethereal drawings show forest scenes, primarily of trees and vegetation common to the woods. In this natural setting the artist has hidden a variety of animals drawn at all angles. The reader will discover creatures up-side-down and at other angles that will necessitate changing the position of the book to find the animal.
    All viewers will be delighted with the book while skills that precede reading are being aided. Young viewers will be captivated by the 100 familiar and hard to find animals.
    (Visual Communication and Classification)

Anno, Mitsumasa. Anno's Journey. Collins and World, 1978.
    Join Anno for a wonderful adventure of the imagination, this time into the realm of people and places. With the artist as your guide you'll meet a fascinating variety of children and adults busy at their work and play, on farms, in villages, or in towns and cities. You will also recognize characters from favorite tales and will see new stories without words unfold from page to page in the tradition of Japanese scroll painting.
    The characteristic art and architecture of northern Europe are pictured in meticulously rendered watercolors and references to great European composers and painters are skillfully included. But look carefully! For, as in all of Anno's books, keen-eyed viewers can also find visual jokes and puzzles as well as tricks of perspective in space and time, extending the imagination of all who travel with him.

Anno, Mitsumasa. The Unique World of Mitsumasa Anno: Selected Works (1968-1977). Philomel Books, 1980.

This unusual book of the art of Mitsumasa Anno will appeal to older children who are familiar with his children's books and to adults who understand not only Anno's artistic genius and wit but also his unique vision of humanity's relationship to science, technology and the arts.

The complex and fascinating world of Anno's art offers the viewer a unique aesthetic experience. Rich in literary and scientific allusion and metaphor, his work not only provides visual delight but also engages the intellect. Each of these 41 paintings is accompanied by a caption, chosen by the artist from relevant works of literature, science and philosophy. Challenging and sometimes enigmatic, the text serves not to explain but rather to complement the art, prodding the viewer to look again and reevaluate the paintings from a new perspective.

Aruego, Jose and Ariane Dewey. We Hide, You Seek. Greenwillow, 1979.

"Let's play. We hide and you seek," the animals say to rhino. Poor, clumsy rhino always manages to find them, but not because he is so clever.

In the bush, he accidentally steps on a kudu's tail; in the desert, he's sidetracked and digs after gerbils; in the swamp, a tickling papyrus makes him sneeze; in the plains, he charges after a butterfly; and when he comes to the river, he falls down the bank. Each time he startles the hidden animals into revealing themselves.

Using the animals of East Africa as protagonists the author/artists not only present an ingenious lesson in camouflage, but provide young viewers with endless hours of delightful seeking and finding.

Benjamin, Alan. 1000 Monsters. Four Winds, 1979.

Here is another spiral-bound flip book whose pages, cut into three parts, allow the reader to mix and match both the text and drawings of monsters. Possibilities exist for 1000 combinations for mix and match monsters and their zany stories. A sequel to the book is available, entitled 1000 Space Monsters Have Landed by Sal Murdocca (Four Winds, 1980).

Billout, Guy. Stone and Steel: A Look at Engineering. Illus. by the author. Prentice-Hall, 1980.

From stone and steel, man has made castles for protection, bridges for crossing, lighthouses for warning and even

a skyscraper for studying. Guy Billout's paintings of the
Chesapeake Bay Bridge and Tunnel, Minot's Ledge lighthouse,
the Cathedral of St. John the Divine and twelve other structures face precisely labelled diagrams showing how each was
built and how each is used. Here is a tribute to man's ingenuity, sure to intrigue those who take the time to really
look!   (Visual Communication)

Briggs, Raymond. The Snowman. Random, 1979.
        The filmstrip-like illustrations in muted pastels tell a
wordless story of a poignant relationship between a small boy
and a snowman. When the boy dreams that his snowman is
real the snowman enters the house and is introduced to modern
appliances and a hot stove. The highly detailed pictures show
how the snowman and the boy each demonstrate the perils and
pleasures of their respective worlds. The book should be
placed in the hands of any child old enough to give attention
to meaning conveyed by pictures.

Brown, Marcia. Listen to a Shape; Touch Will Tell; Walk
        with Your Eyes. Franklin Watts, 1979.
        Here are three separate and revealing visual tours to
help children of all ages toward an awareness of the beauty in
nature. Each is illustrated with stunning photographs. Listen
to a Shape is a poetic interpretation of shapes in nature. It
gives special meaning to the simplest shapes in a child's
world. Touch Will Tell emphasizes all the joys of touch and
feeling, including such touch sensations as soft, fuzzy, delicate and prickles. Walk with Your Eyes shows children how
to use their eyes to walk through a new and different world
and enjoy the simple beauties and wonders of nature.

Cameron, John. If Mice Could Fly. Illus. by the author.
        Atheneum, 1979.
        The author-illustrator presents an imaginative tale of
the relationships of mice and cats in which the mice are
dreaming of fanciful ways to elude the cats while the cats are
realistic in their pursuit of the mice.
        The story leads the reader through the flights of imagi-
nation of the mice. They dream of growing wings and nonchalantly flying just outside the grasp of the cats.
        The clever and inventive cats are steadfast in their
attempt to catch the mice at any price. The mice manage to
outsmart the cats.

The visual communication is highly amusing and imaginative. The reader experiences the competitiveness and determination of the two creatures. The illustrations are vitally important to the story. The text merely suggests the action while the drawings bring out the conflict and excitement.
(Visual Communication)

Carew, Jan. Children of the Sun. Illus. by Leo and Diane Dillon. Little Brown, 1980.
The story concerns two brothers, children of the Sun and a beautiful mortal woman, who are sent by their father on a quest that will allow them to discover the values each would choose to live by. As they travel, their personalities, one trustworthy, the other deceitful, come into conflict and one brother slays the other. Seeing this tragedy, their father, the Sun, intervenes and revives the dead son. The result of the Sun's action is the climax of this tale. Numerous myths are blended into a symbolic whole and the illustrations must be pored over again and again for their haunting, mystic quality and their symbolic representation.

Charlip, Remy and Jerry Joyner. Thirteen. Four Winds, 1975.
In thirteen double-page spreads thirteen separate stories are developed. The unusual format will inspire all ages to compare objects, watch the changing reflections and find new visual experiences. The development of the book can serve as a model to young artist/storytellers as well. Charlip and Joyner exchanged drawings regularly, adding and embellishing each other's work as each of the thirteen stories developed. Neither knew what the other would add next, so the surprise ending of each story was a surprise to the authors as well! The graphic variety allows unlimited possibilities for the simple stories to be expanded, pondered over and discussed for meaning.

Demi. Where Is It? Illus. by the author. Doubleday, 1980.
In still another (and more difficult) hide-and-seek book, the author/artist challenges the young viewer to study carefully the small inserts on the pages and find similar figures hidden among a collage of clowns, birds, fish, etc. The illustrations are deliberately confusing and finding the match is not always easy. A key is provided for unsuccessful searchers.

Fisher, Aileen. <u>Anybody Home</u>? Illus. by Susan Bonners.
    Crowell, 1978.
       The small nook that a young child discovers in the
meadow near her house contains a mouse's nest, the secret
burrow beneath a rock, a fox's den, the hollow tree, a rac-
coon's house. How she wishes she could look inside to see
the animals in their homes!
       In this poem, Aileen Fisher, winner of the 1978 Na-
tional Council of Teachers of English Award for Poetry for
Children, once again evokes the wonder all young children
feel toward the world of nature. Susan Bonner's drawings
bring children right inside the cozy nesting places of favorite
and familiar animals.

Goodall, John S. <u>An Edwardian Season</u>. Atheneum, 1980.
       In a succession of beautifully detailed, exquisitely
painted watercolors, the author/artist has caught the essence
of the Edwardian "Season," during which rich and aristocratic
families came to stay in London for three months to be near
the royal court. Dancing at a coming-out ball, attending a
performance at the Royal Opera House in Convent Garden,
watching a cricket match at Lord's, going to the Rose Show
or a Buckingham Palace garden party--these are some of the
many delights that filled the season. This now-vanished time
is pictured in all its elegance in this book without words.

Goodall, John. <u>The Story of an English Village</u>. Atheneum,
    1979.
       In this visual tour of social history the artist shows
the changes that take place in an English village as it grows
from a clearing in medieval times to a bustling town in modern times. Half pages, ingeniously used, continually alter
the scene and unroll a pageant of history, without words. The
castle, the church and the market cross survive to some ex-
tent down the centuries. So do the road, which becomes a
street, and the house on its corner, whose interior changes
as social patterns change. The scene is depicted from the
same viewpoint at intervals of roughly one hundred years from
the 14th century to the 20th century. A truly challenging
visual tour!

Goodall, John S. <u>Victorians Abroad</u>. Illus. by the author.
    Atheneum, 1981.
       Here is another magnificent visual tour by Goodall,

this time during the reign of Queen Victoria when travel was a favorite pastime. The Victorians made leisurely and extensive journeys to all parts of the world, despite the inconveniences and occasional hazards they encountered. They frequented such fashionable cities and resorts on the continent of Europe as Venice, Deauville, Pompeii, and Nice. They sailed on the Nile, explored Africa, attended viceregal garden parties in India, spent warm weather months in Kashmir, enjoyed long sea voyages. In this wordless book the artist shows us scenes and vignettes from these earlier times so vividly and in such detail that it is hard to believe he was not himself a Victorian abroad. (Visual communication)

Hutchins, Pat. Changes, Changes. Illus. by the author.
      Macmillan, 1971.
      An active and colorful wordless book showing the many uses blocks of wood can have. The story moves along rapidly from page to page with the excitement of the action growing in the mind of the reader. The two cheerful and resourceful characters in the story are active and industrious in their use of the blocks in telling a story of skill and ingenuity.
      The book presents a subtle but true thought that changes are ever present and necessary. The young reader who can grasp this thought or concept and can see the need to accept and execute change will experience growth in many areas.
      (Visual communication)

Isadora, Rachel. Ben's Trumpet. Greenwillow Books, 1979.
      The story of Ben is fiction, but it could be the story of more than one jazz musician who grew up in the twenties. Using the art-deco style of the period, the artist not only captures the poignancy and yearning of youthful talent, but in page after page the use of pattern and shape and form seems to convey the very sound of music. A visual tour into the world of music for children and adults alike.

Lasker, David. The Boy Who Loved Music. Illus. by Joe
      Lasker. Viking, 1979.
      Karl, the boy who loves music, is a horn player in the orchestra of Prince Nicolaus Esterhazy. But Karl loves his family, too, and as the autumn drags on, the Prince lingers at his favorite summer castle, Esterhaza, keeping his unhappy musicians away from family and friends in Vienna. No one can persuade the Prince to leave, until Joseph Haydn,

the Prince's famous director, composes a new symphony with
an ususual ending.

The Boy Who Loved Music is filled with visual delight,
from the interpretation of the misery of the musicians to the
surprise of the Prince at the unusual symphony. The artist
has carefully recreated the customs and fashions of eighteenth-
century Europe. There is much here for children to discover.

Livermore, Elaine. Lost and Found. Houghton Mifflin, 1975.

This is a puzzle book for the very young. Using the
device of a bird turned thief, the author/illustrator creates
pairs of matching pictures. In the second pair an object has
been removed. The objects are always present but not obviously so. An answer page at the end of the book will help
young viewers who have trouble searching through the intricate
figures and backgrounds.

Macaulay, David. Unbuilding. Illus. by the author. Houghton Mifflin, 1980.

Constructing the Empire State Building--eighty-six
floors of steel, concrete, limestone and glass--was an in-
credible feat of engineering science. But the "unbuilding" of
such a structure offers an even more demanding challenge.

The author/artist, with superb draftsmanship and impish
humor, orchestrates the skills of a myriad of specialists as
the scaffolding rises, the rubble chutes are set in place, and
the step-by-step dismantling of an American landmark begins.
Watching the great skyscraper's demolition, the reader comes
to realize the precise timing and organization involved in such
a task.

Never again will we see the Empire State Building in
the same way, for in his carefully researched, meticulous account of how it might be unbuilt, David Macaulay has provided an exciting new perspective on the most characteristic
form of American architecture.

MacLachlan, Patricia. Through Grandpa's Eyes. Illus. by
Deborah Ray. Harper & Row, 1980.

The gentle text and soft illustrations reveal the world
of the senses of touch, smell, hearing and taste as a little
boy and his grandfather explore the world. Grandpa, who is
blind, is a keen observer of the world around him. He knows
the sound of song sparrows and Canada Geese, the smell of
marigolds and fresh paint, and even knows that his grandson

needs a haircut when he tucks him into bed. This is a beautiful reminder that there are many ways to experience the world around us.

Moore, Clement. The Night Before Christmas. Illus. by
Tomie dePaola. Holiday House, 1980.
This new edition of an old favorite is truly a visual tour for children. The illustrations are among the few that are actually faithful to the text. Since St. Nicholas is described as a "right jolly old elf," the artist has made him elflike, and shows him driving a miniature sleigh with eight tiny reindeer. The poem is set in a mid-nineteenth-century New England town and the many patterns and borders throughout the book are based on designs from New England quilts.

Newell, Peter. Topsys and Turveys. Dover, 1964.
The author-artist of this invertible picture-verse collection was a turn-of-the-century illustrator and a leading popular artist in experimental techniques. The trick of topsy-turvey is that each drawing is actually two. Turn to any page of the book; the drawing you will see will have a caption beneath it. Turn the book upside-down and another drawing and caption emerge to complete the tale. The seventy-four topsy-turveys in this collection provide graphic examples of the art of perspective.

Oxenbury, Helen. 729 Curious Creatures. 729 Puzzle People.
729 Merry Mix-Ups. Harper and Row, 1979.
It's possible to put together 729 impossible animals, 729 zany people and 729 caricatures of all sorts with these three books by author/artist Helen Oxenbury. Young readers can combine pictures of heads, bodies, and legs and the words that go with them in 2,187 hilarious ways. Each page is divided into three segments that turn independently. The resulting mix-up of pictures and text is a visual delight sure to give new perspective of image and shape to the young viewer.

Siedelman, James E. and Mintoyne, Grace. The 14th Dragon.
Illustrations by Robert L. Anderson, Victoria Chess,
Nicole Claveloux, Virginia Fritz, Edward Gorey, Donald
Leake, Stan Mack, Robert Nedler, John Norman, Jr.,
Ralph Pinto, Paul Spina, Pat Stewart, Murray Tinkle-
mann. A Harlan Quist Book, 1968.

Bold black and white silhouettes of a hunting party of fourteen members begin a dragon hunt. Each page reveals a different dragon illustrated by a different artist. The dragons are all unique in shape and personality, yet all are bizarre and bright.

As each dragon appears, a hunter quickly claims it for his own and the two leave the scene together. The hunting party dwindles one by one until only the smallest hunter is left without a dragon of his own. Resourcefully, he gets paper and crayons and sits down to create his very own dragon --dragon number fourteen.

The book is a springboard for creativity--who could resist creating his very own dragon? The young reader can understand the desire to take your dragon home once you've found him. A marvelous activity book for young readers and artists. The concept of seriation is seen as the dragons increase in number and the hunting party decreases in size.

(Visual Communication)

Smith, Mr. and Mrs. The Long Dive. Atheneum, 1979.
The unusual full color art and spare text provide an excellent opportunity for the viewer to verbalize visual images. Three friends, Barley the lamb, Jacko the puppet monkey, and Teddy the toy bear, are at the seaside. Suddenly Barley falls from the cliff where they stand, down into the ocean. In an attempt at rescue the other two friends follow. In a moment all three animals are deep in the sea. Much of what they (and the reader) see there is beautiful and exciting: luminous fish, bevies of mermaids, fascinating grottos. But some of it is scary: a large crab, an octopus and a fast submarine.

This is a perfect introduction for young children to the wonders of deep sea life, both real and imaginary. What a challenge to distinguish between the two!

Schaaf, Peter. An Apartment House Close Up. Four Winds, 1980.
We've all seen apartment houses, but how many of us have taken the time to look at one close up? In beautiful duotone photographs Peter Schaaf explores an apartment house, showing us the doors, hallways, rooms and windows from inside and out. Along the way he reveals such mysteries of daily life as where the heat, water, gas and electricity comes from, where the garbage goes and how the elevator works. This is not only an intimate portrait of a familiar place for

From An Apartment
House Close Up, by
Peter Schaaf.

many children but is also a thought-provoking book about people and how they live.

Spier, Peter. People. Illus. by the author. Doubleday,
    1980.
        Here is a true celebration of life with all its diversity.
In this panoramic view of multicultural concepts, the author-
illustrator challenges young people to see, to compare, to
analyze and to create. This is a varied and detailed look at
the world's people, lands and customs. It is also a book of
lively contrasts which challenge stereotyped views of other
cultures. The many uses of the book in gifted programs can
best be described through teachers' and children's reactions
to it. (Page numbers were assigned to allow children to respond to that part of the book which had the most appeal).
The questions that follow were developed by Nancy Karl, teacher in the Francis Howell School District, Mo.

Questions

1. Choose one of the noses on page five. Write a character sketch of the person to whom the nose belongs.

   A ten-year-old writes:
   "This is Mr. Longhead. He gets his name because he has a long chin, head and nose. He is a champion critic. He has won ten awards for criticizing people. His favorite hobby is sharpening his nose with a pencil sharpener." (Shona Bratton)

2. On page seven, choose one of the countries pictured by the clothing worn there. Look in other resource books to discover why the people dress as they do. Create or design new clothing for the people based on your research.

3. Pages eleven and twelve picture games played all over the world. Choose one of the games and research the origin. Compare the game with a similar game played in our country.

4. Select one of the homes pictured on pages thirteen and fourteen. Pretend you are vacationing there. Write a letter to your parents describing the home and the people who live there.

   Corky writes:

   Dear Mom and Dad,
   I'm enjoying the Antarctic. Today I went seal hunting. I didn't catch one, but Papik did. Then we moved to a new camp since hunting and fishing wasn't too good. When we got near a river we pitched camp. Papik's Dad, Milak, started to make an igloo.
   He took his knife and cut some fresh snow into blocks. Then Papik stacked them from the outside. Finally they met at the top and Milak was inside the igloo with no door! When Fatik, Papik's mother, decided where to put the door, Milak cut his way out. For supper we had whale meat. Yuck! Papik, Milak, and Fatik gobbled it down.
   Finally, it was time for bed. With four blankets

I was cozy as a polar bear. I'll come back soon.

Love,
Corky

5. Select one of the twelve holidays pictured on page eighteen. Research the origin of the holiday with a partner. Make posters telling about the coming of your holiday.

6. Write a job description for one of the occupations on page twenty-three. Interview your classmates for the job. Does anyone qualify for the position?

Jenny Dishian writes:

Occupation: Circus Clown
Description: A happy person who can communicate with people of all kinds. Someone who can make people laugh. A person who can juggle and who is very flexible.
Questions to be asked in an interview:
a. Do you like children?
b. Do you enjoy making people laugh?
c. Can you juggle?
d. Can you do acrobatics?
e. Do you have strong legs?
f. What is your idea of a good clown?
g. Do you like to travel?
h. Are you allergic to any kind of animal?

7. You are a news reporter for the Daily News. Write an article to accompany one of the pictures on page twenty-four. Assume it is the front-page article in today's edition. You are limited to fifty words. What will you say?

Tom Henley writes: City Ashamed of Ghetto

The city has started a clean-up job on the ghetto just inside the city limits. The people living in the area are upset because the property is going to the pits, as one resident said. In any case, the clean-up job will be a big one.

8. Practice the sign language on page twenty-six.

Communicate with your classmates using sign language. Rewrite a familiar radio or television commercial in sign language. Rewrite a nursery rhyme in sign language.

9. On pages thirty-one and thirty-two select one of the people who have contributed something for which they are remembered. Write a biographical sketch of that person. Compile and publish a class book of biographies.

10. List the advantages and disadvantages of living in the dreadfully dull city on pages thirty-six and thirty-seven. Compare and contrast it with the exciting and colorful city on the following pages.
Select ten things in the picture and list them on a card. Exchange cards with a classmate and find the items on the list.

Other student reactions to these questions included colorful holiday posters, hamburger commercials in sign language, biographical sketches, and unusual clothing designs. For each question the children observed, analyzed, researched relevant data and used the information in the creation of a new product.

Taber, Anthony. Cat's Eyes. Illus. by the author. E. P. Dutton, 1978.
The cover tells us, "This is how the world looks to a cat, from the cat's eye level of ten inches off the floor. Or at least to one cat in particular, a striped fellow named Tiger. This is Tiger's story."
This is a book of few words, delightfully illustrated in soft black and white drawings that take the child through the life of Tiger, from birth to death. Children will be fascinated by this easy reader that is as much fun as a basket of kittens. This book is an excellent example of the concept of point of view. We truly do not all see the same things at the same time!

Taborin, Glorina. Norman Rockwell's Counting Book. Crown Publishers, 1977.
The child introduced to the wonderful world of numbers

through this very special counting book can truly count his blessings, for he will also discover the wonderful world of artist Norman Rockwell. It is a world of fact and fantasy, of children and grownups, of seriousness and humor, of every-day and holiday. As a marvelous visual tour, the book is a key not only to numbers but to people and objects and colors as well. The last three pictures in the book are reproductions of April Fool's Day paintings filled with mistakes. How many children can find all one hundred fifty-one errors? They are there for the visually literate to see!

Turpin, Lorna. The Sultan's Snakes. Illus. by the author. Greenwillow, 1980.

Here is a delightful book for sharp-eyed viewers! The Sultan's slinky, brightly patterned and friendly snakes disappear one day after deciding to fool the Sultan. Not being as visually literate as the reader, the Sultan can't find a single snake. But children will delight in spotting them on every page, disguised as belts, handles on water jugs, the spout on a coffee pot and in dozens of other positions! This is a visual tour for even the youngest child!

Weil, Lisl. Owl and Other Scrambles. Dutton, 1980.

From airplane to zebra, find the word spelled in the picture. This inventive alphabet book is a puzzle, a visual and verbal game. Many of the puzzles can be solved by pre-schoolers. The alphabet appears on each page and is color-keyed to the beginning letter of the scrambled word.

Wildsmith, Brian. Puzzles. Illus. by the author. Franklin Watts, 1970.

A fantastic and colorful collection of questions that will delight the mind of the young reader. The questions and an-swers are found on the same page amid an abundance of color and creativity.

A mother hen is shown with three broken egg shells and two fluffy yellow chicks. The question is asked, "How many chicks should this mother hen have?" All counting readers can respond to this question in a positive manner. Another page is covered with colorful geometric shapes. The question is, "Which color do you like best?" The decision may take time but all answers will be correct.

The reader is challenged to observe and make deci-sions for each page. The illustrations are as varied as the

colors used to attract the reader to the pages. Brian Wildsmith presents a book of mind-expanding questions in a game-
like manner that will delight and stimulate the imagination of
most children in a positive way. (Visual communication)

Wolkstein, Diane. White Wave, A Chinese Tale. Illus. by
Ed Young. Crowell, 1979.
One evening a lonely Chinese farmer finds a snail
shell gleaming in the moonlight. The shell transforms his
life, for when he brings it home, he discovers it is the house
of the beautiful moon goddess, White Wave. In this touching
tale of the poor farmer and the goddess many truths about
life are revealed, but only the very astute will find each level
of truth.
Illustrator Ed Young takes one through a breathtaking
tour of White Wave as the form of the snail shell rolls wave-
like from one page to the next, always present yet never in-
truding. Then, too, only the child with a very keen sense
of detail will see the similarity in shape (and symbolic meaning) of the hair of the goddess and the top of the shrine which
the farmer built to honor her. White Wave is a book of radi-
ant beauty and wisdom.

Yolen, Jane. The Seeing Stick. Illus. by Remy Charlip and
Demetra Maraslis. Thomas Y. Crowell, 1977.
The ancient city of Peking is the setting for this tale
from Chinese folklore. The emperor's lovely daughter is surrounded with wealth and beauty, yet all the treasures of her
father's kingdom fail to bring her pleasure. The girl has
been blind since birth and she cannot visualize the beauty
around her. Her father is hopeful that someone may be able
to help her see. He resolves to reward such a person with
a fortune in jewels. Men come from far and near but their
prayers, incantations and potions all fail to make the princess
see.
An old man in a distant village hears of her problem
and begins his journey to help the emperor's daughter. He
carries with him his walking stick made of golden wood and
his whittling knife. As he journeys to the palace he carves
the faces and events he encounters along the way. Everyone
is impressed with the carvings on the walking stick. When
the princess hears of the wondrous walking stick she begs to
touch it. The old man tells her it is not a walking stick but
a seeing stick.
Up to this point in the story the illustrations have been

in somber black and white but as the old man begins to tell the girl of his journey he introduces each event, character and object, while the princess follows by touching the intricate carving on the stick. The illustrations begin to unfold in color as the girl uses her fingers to see. What had once been a sad princess has changed to one filled with joy and a desire to learn more about the world around her.

The emperor fulfills his promise to reward anyone bringing sight to his daughter. The Princess now teaches the blind children of Peking how to see with their finger tips as the old man taught her. The seeing stick has opened a new world for the blind Princess. The old man knew the joy she felt: the seeing stick had brought joy to his life for he too was blind.

CHAPTER 3

PICTURE BOOKS AND COMMUNICATION SKILLS

One of the first acts of a totalitarian government is to take away the books of the society it controls. Why? Simply put, removing the books is the first step toward the simplification of language, and as language becomes simple, so does thought.

Our goal for all children is literacy. More instructional time is spent on increasing children's ability to communicate ideas, information and experiences than in any other area of instruction. The goal of literacy is to help each child reach an acceptable level of competence in understanding and using language in both oral and written form.

All free societies value the growth and development of the communication skills of their peoples, yet modern technology developed for the masses has had an adverse affect on the individual's ability to communicate.

The average television program provides a ready example of over-simplification of speech, content and theme. The viewing process itself pre-empts individual communication and eliminates the need (or the desire) for reading. It is a passive medium which requires little in the way of creative thought or interpretation from the viewer. Its common images deaden the imagination (all western marshals look like Matt Dillon) and distort reality. Yet it is the form of communication most used today by young and old alike.

If we are to lure young people away from such media and toward developing their own abilities to communicate, we must make the alternatives very attractive.

The development of communication skills is most likely to take place in a rich environment where written and oral language activities receive top priority. Interest centers, multi-reading areas filled with a wide variety of challenging and exciting books, bulletin board space which allows children to communicate with each other, and ample time for reading and sharing books and creative writing--all these are parts of a literate environment.

It is essential to remember that the greatest, most fluent and exciting writers throughout the history of mankind have left their legacy to us in the pages of books. Our choices in seeking communication models for gifted minds are vast!

How, then, does one find, among the hundreds or thousands of titles available, the very best to share with children? Once again, the answer can be found in the picture book. The execution of a fine picture book is a complex task, as the illustrator-author strives to construct a unified whole that speaks clearly and strongly to the reader. It is this very unity of purpose that facilitates clear and powerful communication and enables the teacher to select easily from many titles those which are most appropriate for the purpose of the moment.

Picture books can serve as powerful and effective models in developing communication skills with gifted students. It is impossible to read challenging and entertaining books without expanding our vocabularies. Concepts are difficult to wrestle with when we have no means of communicating them. Even within, we need words to clarify our thoughts. A child who is deprived of the richness of language is deprived of the greatest tool he can be given to tackle the present and the future.

> Gifted children show a natural affinity and delight with words. From the earliest response to Mother Goose and lullabies to the 'blob of glup' in James Thurber's tongue-teasing The Thirteen Clocks (Simon and Schuster, 1950), language fascinates and lures them. What child hasn't shivered deliciously when Zorn of Zorna was threatened to be slit from his 'guggle' to his 'zatch!' (From Reading Guidance in a Media Age)

Words can foretell of infinite delight as well as infinite meaning.

> This is Susie. If she's building her sand castle right next to yours, you're in a POTENTIAL TROU-

> BLE SPOT. That means Susie's digging might clog
> your moat, creating an INCIDENT. If you yell,
> 'move!' You have a DISPUTE!

These opening lines from Louise Armstrong's How to Turn
War into Peace (Harcourt, 1979) challenge young readers of
various ages to anticipate the use of concept clusters related
to war and peace as two children attempt to build sand castles
on the same beach.

   Children are natural poets, and when exposed either to
the fluid beauty of genuine poetry or to nonsense verse, they
respond with even keener adeptness in their own communica-
tions.   Still in tune with the living poetry of wind, sea and
sky, they share with us such gems as "Mr. Rain telephoned
Mr. Sun by lightning to tell him the storm was over."

   In comparing and contrasting variations of picture book
folk tales all critical thinking skills are called into play.   In
examining new versions of familiar tales the child must be
open-minded to new ideas and realize that other cultures have
different ideas about the meanings of words.   The child questions things that don't make sense and learns to separate emotional from logical thinking.   He or she can analyze similarities and differences and seek to understand their causes.

   Every school library contains a good many books which
can be used to enhance communication skills.   The titles
selected for review here are by no means an inclusive list,
but all were chosen to meet the following criteria:

1.   Books which share delight in the use of language,
     which play with words and serve as models for
     students to use in experimenting with word cate-
     gories, phrases, sentences, stories and poetry.

2.   Books rich in description--of scenes, of charac-
     ters and of feelings.   These books display
     the skill of the author in creating rich visual
     images.

3.   Books which will lead the child to make com-
     parisons among things and to show relationships
     and associations, noting likenesses and differ-
     ences and how ideas might be combined.

4.   Books which foster empathy and provide oppor-

tunities for students to share personal experiences or thoughts that are similar to those of the characters portrayed.

5.   Books which will help the student to become more skillful in interpreting and using nonverbal forms of communication, including the ability to translate from visual to verbal and to compare visual messages.

SUMMARY OF COMMUNICATION SKILLS

(Adapted from "Project Reach," courtesy of Joyce Juntune)

Communication is the ability to express thought and ideas to others and includes the following areas:

1.   Description within categories: the teacher encourages the student to list many words within given categories.
    a.   set categories
    b.   list words
    c.   was words together to write phrases, sentences, stories, poetry, etc.

2.   Description of feelings: the teacher encourages the student to use a variety of words to describe his/her feelings and values.
    a.   use empathy situations as they arise in classroom rather than trying to invent situations
    b.   use pictures of moods and emotions

3.   Comparisons and relationships: the teacher leads the students to make comparisons among things or show relationships and associations.
    a.   it's good for the student to bring two things together for comparison
    b.   he/she asks how they are alike and how they are different
    c.   then he/she determines how they might be put together

4.   Empathy: the teacher builds upon opportunities

for students to share personal experiences or thoughts of others.
a. this is a spontaneous situation
b. it is verbally recognized when observed in students
c. it cannot be pre-planned

5. Non-verbal: the teacher guides the student to become more skillful in interpreting and using non-verbal form of communication to express his/her feelings, thoughts, and needs to others. These are progressive stages:
    a. throw out words and ask children to react with whole body
    b. give situations and ask children to react
    c. list occupations or categories and ask children to strike pose of one and then freeze
    d. in small groups create a circumstance and tell children to play a scene without discussing it with anyone--just look around and find a way to fit in
    e. portray an idea using a symbol

6. Composition: the teacher creates opportunities for the student to organize words into meaningful networks of meanings, thoughts, and needs
        questioning--asks questions about detail, but stays centered on subject

7. Sample warm-ups
    a. Description within given categories
        "One part of communication is using descriptive words. Let's look at this snowball. What words describe how it looks? What words describe how it feels?"
    b. Description of feelings
        "Describe how you feel when you've called all your friends; accurately describe your feelings. "
    c. Comparison/Relationships
        Give each student a cotton ball. "What words can you use to finish this sentence? Cotton is as white as ......"
    d. Empathy
        Empathy does not lend itself to written activity. It is most effectively developed when it is positively reinforced as it occurs in the classroom.

   e. Composition
   "Yesterday the mailman came to my house
   with a huge, gigantic package addressed to
   me. Then what do you think happened?"
   "Suppose you came to class one day and
   found a substitute teacher with no directions
   to follow. Compose, in your own mind,
   what you would need to tell him/her. Be
   sure your ideas are expressed clearly and
   concisely. " Have the students orally give
   the directions as they would give them to
   the substitute.

   f. Non-verbal
   "Show me, using your face, how you feel
   when you eat a foot-long hot dog. Add
   your hands and body to help show. Now
   pretend you have had 35 hot dogs! Show
   how you feel. "

Aardema, Verna. The Riddle of the Drum. Illus. by Tony
   Chen. Four Winds, 1979.
     A palace guard carried a special drum throughout the
land of Tizapan, chanting a strange riddle. For the King
would not give his daughter's hand in marriage unless her
suitor proved himself worthy of her. He had hired a wizard
to make the drum out of a special kind of leather. Then he
sent the guard out to chant the riddle which invited prospec-
tive suitors to guess what the special leather was.
     The drum gave off a sound like thunder on a distant
mountain. A handsome prince from a nearby land heard it,
and decided he would be the one to solve the riddle and win
the princess.
     But solving the riddle wasn't easy. Fortunately the
prince met some very unusual people on his way to Tizapan.
Each had special gifts which were brought into use to help the
prince in his task.
     This is a variant of numerous tales and children who
are familiar with The Fool of the World and the Flying Ship
will begin to make immediate comparisons.
                       (Language-Comparisons)

Andersen, Hans Christian. The Snow Queen. A newly adapted
   version by Naomi Lewis. Illus. by Errol le Cain. The
   Viking Press, 1979.
     "Once in a great town, lived two poor children. They

were not brother and sister, but they were just as fond of each other as if they were. He was called Kay, and she Gerda."

So begins this poignant tale of a girl's quest for her friend. Kay has been enchanted by the wicked Snow Queen who can fly through dark clouds and cover the windows with ice. Through winter and spring, along river and mountain-side, Gerda searches for Kay, who, with his heart frozen, lies asleep at the feet of the Snow Queen in her ice palace.

Errol le Cain's magnificent illustrations are perfect for this Andersen tale, which can be read and discussed on many levels. For young children it is a beautiful example of Andersen's power of description and his creation of imaginary settings, qualities found in few other literary offerings. For older students it is a tale of the power of love and of perseverence, themes which need further exploration in our modern society. (Description)

Banchek, Linda. Snake In, Snake Out. Illus. by Elaine Arnold. Crowell, 1979.
It could happen to anyone's grandmother. This is the up-down-in-out-over-under-off (the only eight words used in the book) story of how a lovable little old lady who unexpectedly finds herself the owner of a snake finally becomes friends with her pet. Wonderful pictures and a few words make this a good choice for a child's retelling.
(Language - Prepositions)

Basil, Cynthia. Breakfast in the Afternoon. Illus. by Janet McCaffery. Morrow, 1979.
Here is a riddle approach to the origin and definitions of selected compound words for early and middle grades. The use of riddles involves the child in the learning process and the bright illustrations enliven the total language experience. (Language - Compound Words)

Blossom, Naomi. A Scale Full of Fish and Other Turnabouts. Greenwillow, 1979.
This delightful introduction to homonyms will challenge young minds to create and illustrate turnabouts of their own. Wood block prints illustrate the diverse meanings of ten pairs of words. Imagine: "A scale full of fish and a fish full of scales." After enjoying the book, children have offered such

additions as: "A girl on a train, a train (wedding) on a girl"
and "A ring on a hand, a hand on a ring (circle). "
(Language - Homonyms)

Chess, Victoria. Alfred's Alphabet Walk. Greenwillow, 1979.
This is a challenging introduction to the alphabet, combining unusual pictures to extend vocabulary and delightful al-
literation to roll off the tongue.
Alfred's mother tells him to stay in the front yard and
learn the alphabet. Alfred does learn the alphabet, but he
doesn't learn it in the front yard--or does he?
As Alfred's imagination soars and creates wonderful,
exotic happenings during his alphabet walk, the imaginations
of young readers will soar as well. (Language - Description)

Clark, Ann Nolan. In the Land of the Small Dragon. Illus.
by Tony Chen. Viking Press, 1979.
In the Land of the Small Dragon there lives a man and his
two daughters, Tam and Cam. Tam, the beautiful and good
child, is made to work hard by her jealous stepmother, who
favors her own child, Cam. But Tam gets help from a fairy
godmother, a fish with magical powers, and the willing forces
of nature. As a reward for her kindness she acquires a beautiful dress and jeweled slippers.
One day a small bird drops one beautiful slipper in
front of the Emperor's son, who is walking in the garden.
The prince decides he must marry the girl whose foot will
fit the lovely slipper.
In traditional metric form and with proverbs inter-
spersed among the verses, Ann Nolan Clark recreates an
authentic Cinderella variation. In searching for similarities
and differences students can be challenged to seek and compare others of the known 347 versions of the classic Cinderella tale. (Literature - Analysis)

Clifton, Lucille. My Friend Jacob. Illus. by Thomas Di-
Grazia. E. P. Dutton, 1980.
Jacob and Sam live next door to each other. They
are very best friends. Sometimes Jacob (the older) helps
Sam (the younger and smaller) do things, like play basketball,
and to learn all the makes of the cars that go by.
Sam helps Jacob, too. Mostly he helps him remember, which is very hard for Jacob. And one day Sam decides
to teach Jacob to do something he's never done before: how
to knock on a door before entering.

Can discerning children with a strong sense of empathy discover the real meaning of the relationship of the two boys? Through a sensitive text and soft illustrations the author and artist lead the reader to conclusions which are never stated verbally. The child's oral interpretation of this story will quickly reveal his level of visual literacy.

(Non-verbal language - Empathy)

Cohen, Barbara. Lovely Vassilisa. Illus. by Anatoly Ivanof. Atheneum, 1980.

This Russian folktale is one of the 347 known variants of the Cinderella story. Lovely Vassilisa's mother is dead and her father is a merchant who travels. Her stepmother and two ugly stepsisters treat her badly when her father is gone. Eventually they send her on an errand to the witch, Baba Yaga. But Vassilisa has a small wooden doll that helps her in time of need, and because of the doll she is able to please Baba Yaga. Through Baba Yaga's efforts, the wicked stepmother and stepsisters die. But it is by her own efforts and the dolls that Vassilisa marries the son of the Tzar.

The comparisons with the Cinderella variants make a fascinating study which will lead children to an awareness of cultures other than their own, and perhaps a better understanding of people of the world. Analysis is a higher-level thinking skill which is essential to the study of folk tale variants. Such a study might well help students develop a healthy curiosity and an urge to dig more deeply into the reasons for the differences. (Language-Comparisons-Relationships)

Corbett, Scott. Jokes to Read in the Dark. Illus. by Annie Gusman. E. P. Dutton, 1980.

"Here lies the body of Wilfred White.
His bullet-proof vest wasn't quite."

With this sobering sample of the author's ability to play with words, the reader is launched into a contagious collection of limericks, puns, epitaphs, knock-knocks, elephant jokes and shaggy-dog stories. There are chucklers, groaners, and jokes that defy categorization. But within each type of humor are found ways to turn, twist, and manipulate words which are sure to fascinate the child who finds special satisfaction in word plays.

Under the guise of instructing his readers in the pitfalls of writing BJs (bad jokes) Scott Corbett has collected the best and worst of his own writing. This is sure to stimulate young jokesters to try their own hands at following the

many models given here.   A final example of epitaph humor
closes the book:
> "Here lies the body of Kermit Smoot,
> (He almost learned to parachute)"
>   (Language: Puns, word plays)

Fisher, Leonard Everett.   The Jetty.   Illus. by the author.
    Viking Press, 1981.
     The spare text and magnificent illustrations by a win-
ner of the Pulitzer painting prize capture a moment in time
and in memory.
> "Low tide and daylight were Levi Farber's tide and
> time.   The Jetty was his place.   There he sat in
> the cockpit of the rocks, watching a lone ship and
> the rolling sea."
     The quiet and gentle mood of the opening lines slowly
changes as "a breeze began to push the clammy air from one
side of the bay to the other."
     Day becomes night as a squall approaches and its wind
and rain drives Levi to shelter.   The boy watches the storm
play itself out over the jetty, which "stands firm as always,"
and he returns to his place of dreams and aspirations, the
"cockpit in the rocks."
     Here is a fine example of descriptive prose at its best
to help young writers and artists capture their own very special places and moments in time.   (Language - Description)

Gwynne, Fred.   The Sixteen Hand Horse.   Illus. by the au-
    thor.   Windmill/Wanderer Books, 1980.
     In the tradition of his two earlier books, A Chocolate
Moose for Dinner and The King Who Rained, Fred Gwynne
has again gathered together homonyms and figures of speech
and defined each visually.   Children will use many of the
examples given here as springboards to their own elaboration
on words in the English language.   They will discover, for
example, that churches have "cannons," and bells that "peel,"
that "Daddy knows a man who fought a suit and lost" and that
"Aunt Mildred reads palms."   (Words - Description)

Kraus, Robert.   Pinchpenny Mouse.   Windmill Books, 1974.
     As an example of satire and literary style Pinchpenny
Mouse is a gem, a social satire on the industrial revolution
authentically illustrated in a tongue-in-cheek style.   Kraus's
use of the cliché with a twist is evident and artist Robert

Byrd's use of old movie stills from How Green Was My Valley and The Informer add a fascinating dimension to the book.
Use Pinchpenny as a vehicle for comparison with informative texts on the industrial revolution. Students will be delighted to see the similarities! (Language - Comparison)

Lobel, Arnold. Gregory Griggs and Other Nursery Rhyme
People. Illus. by the author. Greenwillow, 1979.
Arnold Lobel has brought to life some obscure nursery rhyme characters and has captured their particular plights and follies in his evocative illustrations. The strong rhyming patterns and the imaginative use of language in the selections add to the reading-aloud appeal of this book. Imagine designing twenty-seven different wigs for Gregory Griggs or creating a thistle pile of unsifted thistles. The artist does this and more as imagination reigns! (Language - Description)

Long, Claudia. Albert's Story. Illus. by Judy Glasser.
Delacorte, 1979.
When do children discover that a story has a beginning, middle and end? Albert's story: "He put the thing on his back." Who did what and why comprises a very original story indeed. Albert, however, fails to grasp the idea, the audience sharing what the character cannot. Young children clamored to explain to Albert. Unable to do so, many told their own fuller tales instead. (Language - Structure)

Maestro, Betsy and Giulio. On the Go: A Book of Adjectives.
Crown, 1979.
Despite the contradictory title, this is a delightful introduction to descriptive words. With spare text and blue and red illustrations a man and his elephant are introduced. They are waiting for the circus to open. One word on each page describes the emotion being felt at the time. On the Go should help children to use more descriptive language in their own writing. (Language - Adjectives)

Marceau, Marcel. The Story of Bip. Illus. by the author.
Harper and Row, 1976.
The master of mime has given young readers an allegory to explain the meaning of the art of mime as he practices it. Bip, the hero of the tale, in his desire to be a magician, sprouts wings and rises to soar in the heavens

above the city of Paris. Wanting to communicate his experience to others, but having no words to do so, Bip arrives at
a circus and finds his opportunity. "Slowly my body, legs
and arms, hands and feet, my face, my soul, began to move
in silent outcry."

The influence of the French Impressionists is evident
in Marceau's illustrations, which lift the reader, along with
Bip, to a nonverbal experience of near perfect understanding.
(Language - NonVerbal)

Mother Goose in Hieroglyphicks. Dover Publications, 1973.
Whether you call them hieroglyphics, rebus rhymes or
simply pictures that take the place of words, delightful woodcuts that take on such forms as cats, children, haystacks,
queens, pies, saws, apples, roses and many other forms
present a guessing challenge here.

First published in 1849, this book has been reissued
to help children find in these rhymes and quaint pictures a
happy challenge to their powers of imagination and a model
for writing their own rebus stories. (Language - Style)

Oram, Hiawyn. Skittlewonder and the Wizard. Illus. by
Jenny Rodwell. Dial, 1980.
Once upon a time there was a prince who was so good
at bowling with skittles that everyone called him Skittlewonder.
But one day he lost a match to an evil wizard. "Find my
name and where I live by Christmas or you'll turn into a set
of skittles yourself," the wizard threatens. Skittlewonder's
search takes him through a realm peopled by gypsies, witches,
elves, fairies and bewitched and lovely maidens, reminiscent
at times of The Hobbit, and like The Hobbit, Skittlewonder is
good-natured and has all the help he needs to triumph. Children will enjoy comparing this Scottish folktale to The Hobbit,
as well as to the traditional Rumplestiltskin.
(Language - Comparison)

Pomerantz, Charlotte. The Tamarindo Puppy and Other
Poems. Illus. by Byron Barton. Greenwillow Books,
1980.
Here is a book in two languages that is one book, without translation or device of any kind. The poems are so
cleverly constructed that the child will scarcely realize that
he or she is reading both English and Spanish.

> "Let's buy pan de agua, daughter.
> Pan is bread and agua water.
> Good fresh bread of flour and water
> Good fresh pan de agua, daughter. "

The poems move back and forth with rich sound and context, providing a delightful language experience for the reader. (Language)

Potter, Beatrix. <u>The Tailor of Gloucester</u>. Frederick Warne, n. d.

"In the time of swords and periwigs and full skirted coats with flowered lappets--when gentlemen wore ruffles and gold-laced waistcoats of paduasoy and taffeta--there lived a tailor in Gloucester. "

The opening lines of Beatrix Potter's gem of a book about a poor tailor who lived along with his cat called Simpkin sets the scene for a rich literary delicacy. With today's emphasis on graded vocabulary and simplified language we forget that neither is necessary when reading aloud. This author's facility with words, words that flow from the tongue, words that play and rhyme, and awe the listener, will make even the most reluctant reader perk up ears.

This touching tale of the tailor's predicament and how he is helped by a band of mice would be trite in the hands of any other, but is a must to be shared, particularly with gifted children, for the beauty of its language.

(Language - Description)

Steel, Flora Annie. <u>Tattercoats</u>. Illus. by Diane Good. Bradbury Press, 1976.

Here, for comparison with the French tale of Cinderella, is the old English version. The girl called Tattercoats ran unhappily from the kitchen to find her friend, the gooseherd. He was her only companion, an odd, magical chap who, when Tattercoats was hungry or cold or tired, would play to her so gaily on his little pipe that she would forget her troubles and dance.

Perhaps he would play to her now. More than anything, she wished she could see the grand doings at the King's ball, where this very night the Prince was to select his bride. But she had merely tatters from the ragbag to wear and had been left home by her bitter old grandfather, who had already set off for the festivities.

The gooseherd knew just what to do. "Take fortune when it comes, little one, " he said, reaching for her hand

and starting her on her way to the King's ballroom. There, before the King and the Prince and all the lords and ladies, the gooseherd played again a magical tune so that everyone saw Tattercoats for herself.

(Language - Comparisons - Relationships)

Timmermans, Gommaar. The Little White Hen and the Emperor of France. Addison-Wesley, 1976.

This parody of history and of human nature may appear at first glance to be a comic book. But don't be fooled: it is a delightful and thoughtful fable that can be read and enjoyed on many levels.

It is the story of a contented farmer and his friend, Blanche, a white hen. Blanche helps John Sprout with all his chores, and together they plant, cultivate and harvest the crops.

But fate intervenes! Far away, in Russia, the forces of war gather. The Emperor of France declares war on the Czar of all Russia, and Blanche is drafted into the Emperor's army as a beast of burden.

Since Blanche must go off to war, John Sprout decides to go with her. The ridiculous situations which follow form a social satire centered on war, government and military structure. For older students, this book can serve as an excellent model in the literature of social satire.

(Language - Style)

Tremain, Ruthven. Teapot, Switcheroo and Other Silly Word Games. Greenwillow, 1979.

Here is a variety of word games for middle grades, especially challenging for gifted classes. Rather than forcing standard workbook exercises on children who handle language well, try these word games which involve homonyms, root words, pig latin, palindromes and spoonerisms.

(Language - Word Games)

Tresselt, Alvin. White Snow, Bright Snow. Illus. by Roger Duvoisin. Lothrop, 1948.

Here, the Caldecott winning author/illustrator team turns the familiar scene of a snowy day into the unique, through Tresselt's use of metaphorical language. The effects of a heavy snow are described, with "automobiles looking like big fat raisins buried in snowdrifts" or "houses crouched together, their windows peeking out from under great white eyebrows."

To share and draw attention to the imagery the author has created is a first important step in helping children understand the importance of using language creatively.

(Language - Description)

Wersba, Barbara. Twenty-Six Starlings Will Fly Through Your Mind. Illus. by David Palladini. Harper and Row, 1980.

"It begins with something to climb on and ends with a dazzling Z. It begins with A, secret and determined. The guide."

The subject is the alphabet, and the guide who leads us into its labyrinth is followed by bandits and balloons, tigers, acrobats, puppets, a woman trailing garnets, clowns drinking marigold wine, and romantic ladies writing impossible poetry.

Here is a truly magnificent tour into the world of words, images and colors. Revealing for the reader a new way of looking at familiar things, it reaches out to the imagination and challenges the thought processes of young and old alike.

Not intended as a concept or vocabulary building book, it does a superb job of building both. Even junior high students may have to ponder the idea that:

"W wanders the woodlands.
He thinks that whimsey and wantonness
takes the same path."

(Language - Description)

Wiesman, Bernard. Morris Has a Cold. Dodd-Mead, 1979.

Here is a marvelous example of the fun of playing with language for young readers. Morris the Moose has a "walking" (not running) nose. He refuses to have his forehead felt because he insists he has just one head. He is fortunate to have Boris the Bear for a friend, for Boris forebears Morris' faux pas (to say nothing of hoofs). The jokes in the story, both verbal and visual, are right on target for any reader old enough to enjoy the word play.

(Language - Literal Interpretation)

CHAPTER 4

BOOKS TO CHALLENGE PRODUCTIVE THINKING

> The present belongs to the sober, the cautious,
> the routine-prone, but the future belongs to those
> who do not rein in their imaginations.
> --Kornei Chukovsky

Imagination and fantasy are vital ingredients for a full
and rich life. They poke fun at reality, play with it, sharpen
it, and eventually illuminate it. The daily routine of required
pursuits tends to squelch the creative spirit. In education,
an over-emphasis on content and convergent responses has
stimulated an assembly-line approach to learning where like
responses are desired, encouraged and rewarded.

By their very nature, fine picture books can nurture
and stimulate creative thought. The child who meets fluency
and flexibility of ideas in the picture book can be challenged
to become fluent in the production of his or her own ideas,
whether they concern the solving of a real problem or the
creation of a work of art or literature. The future of mankind may well depend on the creative and imaginative minds
nourished in our classrooms. Books which challenge productive thinking are essential ingredients, therefore, not only in
gifted programs but in all of education.

Fluency and Flexibility

The most basic of all productive and critical thinking
skills emphasized and developed in gifted programs are fluency
and flexibility. Only when one can produce a large quantity
of original responses will creative new solutions be found in
such areas as social interaction, economic instability, environmental control, foreign relations, and a host of other problems which beset our society.

Children must be exposed to a wide variety of examples of fluent and flexible thinking, including books which contain rich and descriptive language to bring alive objects or events; books which offer a number of solutions to a particular problem; books which play with combining ideas in new and fresh ways, and books which challenge both the visual and mental capabilities of the child.

In addition to the fluent production of ideas the child can be challenged to play with ideas, changing them into new and different forms. Thinking can be stretched so that the child sees associations and classifications within broad generalizations. For example, in Mary Ann Hoberman's delightful book, A House Is a House for Me (Viking 1977), the author begins with the concept of house as a shelter for people. As the rollicking verse builds, the child discovers houses for animals, shelter for machines, the concept of house as a covering ("a glove is a house for a hand"), and the added concept of house as a container ("a teapot is a house for tea"). As Hoberman adds each new category in her development of the idea of houses, the child's thinking stretches and stretches.

The child who acquires the skills of fluent and flexible thinking will be able to examine and develop many points of view and to shift direction in thinking when a solution appears not to work. This child will explore many ways of looking at an object or an idea and will often interpret a written passage or picture very differently from the average child. Books which stimulate this kind of thought will benefit not only the reader but, ultimately, all others who may be touched by his or her life. The concept of flexibility infers the ability to transfer learning from one area to another as well as the incorporation of divergent thinking into the task at hand.

While the books of Richard Scarry have often been criticized by reviewers for their lack of literary merit, few can compete with this talented author/illustrator for fluency of ideas. The very young child who is exposed to books like The Great Big Air Book will have a mind-expanding, language development experience no language-arts text can provide. The same experience can come from many of the books of Peter Spier, whose attention to minute, authentic detail in his classics, London Bridge Is Falling Down and The Fox Went Out on a Chilly Night, should capture the minds and imagination of young children for hours.

Mitsumasa Anno, in addition to challenging the child's ability to see detail in his Anno's Journey and Anno's Italy, is one of the most fluent and flexible illustrators working today. Both books are nearly perfect examples of the fluent and flexible thinker at work. The fluent thinker will find many ways to use a particular object. Anno uses street signs in his illustrations to instruct, to amuse, to puzzle and to draw the viewer through Anno's Journey. One sign is a bottle which gradually empties as pages are turned. Another sign contains opening bars of a Beethoven symphony. Still other signs are filled with historical or economic information, but the information comes from the Shape of the sign. What child taking this journey with Anno could not help but be challenged to fluent and flexible thought!

Originality

Closely related to fluency and flexibility is originality, the ability to produce novel, uncommon or unique responses. The original thinker uses stored information in the formation of new patterns, approaches or ideas. Everything we read or experience is enhanced by everything else we have read and experienced. We could liken the consciousness of each child to a giant jigsaw puzzle with pieces missing here and there. Each experience with a challenging, original picture book may perhaps fit a missing piece of understanding into the whole and at the same time stretch young minds toward original thought of their own.

Perhaps because so few programs were in existence ten years ago, few educators of the gifted have become acquainted with one of the most original of picture book authors. In his Arm in Arm (Four Winds, 1969) Remy Charlip provides an experience in word play using puns, riddles, mirror images, dramatic playlets and free verse poems, all of which bear the shape of their ideas and contribute toward creating a concentrated, imaginative awareness of language. If one accepts the premise that words are the basic tools of thought, books which require verbal gymnastics should be among the first choices of teachers of the gifted.

Arnold Lobel combines all of the productive thinking skills in his outlandish aviary of rare and ridiculous birds entitled The Ice Cream Cone Coot and Other Rare Birds (reissued by Four Winds, 1980). Using easily recognized objects like ice cream cones and electric plugs, the author-

artist has created such unusual fowls as the Garbage Canary
("who lives in conditions quite unsanitary") and the Key Crane
("over our heads the Key Cranes are flocking / looking for
doors that might need unlocking"). Lobel challenges the reader to look at common objects in a totally different way, yet
each of his unusual birds is valuable as an art work alone,
and can lift and mold the child's appreciation of art.

Elaboration

     Elaboration is the thinking skill involved in adding to
or expanding upon an object or an idea in order to make the
original more interesting or workable. The elaborative thinker is rarely satisfied with the status quo. This child will
write more, draw more or add more ideas to a plan, object
or situation. This is the student who is rarely satisfied with
the simplistic solution but who senses a deeper meaning and
works to modify previously accepted approaches or plans.

     Numerous picture book authors are known for their
ability to take an idea and elaborate on it. Tomie DePaola,
in his series of picture books on scientific topics, presents
basic information on the subject, then richly enhances the
text with a parallel story told in pictures which expand the
central idea. Examples of his books which do this so well are
The Quicksand Book, Charlie Needs a Cloak, The Cloud Book,
The Popcorn Book.

     William Pène Dubois, in his Mother Goose for Christ-
mas, takes the simple Mother Goose characters and develops
a picture book which can be employed on many levels. In
Fortunately, Remy Charlip once again plays with words, show-
ing how a story can be developed from two simple words,
"Fortunately" and "Unfortunately." Masters of the parody are
Raymond Briggs (Jim and the Beanstalk) and George Mendoza
(Wart Snake in a Fig Tree).

     Robert Kraus's elaboration of the cliché is the essence
of many of his picture books. A study of the Kraus genius
giving the time-honored cliché an amusing twist is an idea
for gifted programs in the upper elementary, and junior high
school. The best of the Kraus titles for such a study include
Leo the Late Bloomer, Pinchpenny Mouse and Noel the Coward.

Evaluation

The evaluation process requires making a determination about the desirability or undesirability of an object or idea. It is a way of examining an object or a problem or solution to determine the usefulness or desirability of incorporating it into one's plan or lifestyle. In evaluating, students are required to rate, select, decide, or judge. It is a process concerned with the weighing of ideas.

Many, many picture books are appropriate for stimulating evaluation activities. As talented authors pose problems for their characters, they are in essence posing the problems for the reader. As a character chooses, so must the reader evaluate the choice by weighing all aspects of the situation and deciding finally whether to agree or disagree with the character.

In his book, Would You Rather, John Burningham challenges the reader to numerous choices. "Would you rather be made to eat spider stew, slug dumplings, mashed worms or drink snail squash?" In a more serious vein, Richard Kennedy tells of life in The Lost Kingdom of Karnica, which was never the same after Farmer Erd unearthed a valuable red stone in his field. The wise man warns that if the stone is removed, the kingdom will be destroyed, "for the stone is the heart of the kingdom." To remove the stone or not: that is the choice the reader will make along with the inhabitants of the kingdom.

In the section which follows, a summary of productive thinking processes is provided, together with a brief listing of picture books and general strategies for their use in developing productive thinking. The remainder of the section presents books which are especially useful in developing these skills. While it is difficult to point out only one specific productive thinking skill, to the exclusion of others which must certainly be present in a fine children's book, every effort has been made to classify titles by grouping them according to their major function in the development of productive thought.

PRODUCTIVE THINKING (SUMMARY)

Productive thinking involves the following processes:

1. Fluency--Many responses for a given situation. The
   emphasis is on quantity rather than quality.
   For example:
   List many ways to ....
   Think of several possible ways to ....
   Come up with ideas for ....

2. Flexibility--Thinking in a variety of categories by shifting
   thinking from one way into different avenues or ways of
   thinking.
   For example:
   List many different kinds of ways to ....
   Think of different kinds of reasons for ....
   What are the different kinds of ....

3. Originality--Expressing unusual or uncommon responses--
   clever and unique ideas that are relevant but a departure
   from the obvious.
   For example:
   Think of ideas no one else will think of ....
   Think of unique and unusual ways to ....

4. Elaboration--Elaborate upon a basic idea by adding details
   to make it more interesting and complete.
   For example:
   Add supplemental ideas to make the basic idea clearer.
   Think of details to add to your main idea.

5. Evaluation--Weighing ideas in terms of the desirability
   and undesirability of each.
   For example:
   List the things that you like and dislike about ....
   List the pros and cons of ....
   In order to lessen prejudice towards an idea, strive to
   equalize the number of likes and dislikes/pros and cons.

Sample Activities--Productive Thinking

Aruego, Jose. Look What I Can Do. Charles Scribner's
    Sons, 1971.
        Fluency: List several things you can do.
        Flexibility: List different kinds of things you can do.
        Originality: List something you can do that you think
                     very few of your friends can do.
                     Tell something unusual you would like to
                     do.

Baker, Alan. Benjamin and the Box. Lippincott, 1977.
Before the secret of the box is revealed, ask the
children:
Fluency: What could possibly be in the box?
Originality: What other ways might Benjamin try to
open the box?

Behrens, June. What I Hear. Childrens Press, 1976.
Fluency: List several things you hear at home.
Flexibility: List the different kinds of sounds you
hear in a day.
Originality: Tell about the most unusual sound you
have ever heard.

DuBruyn, Monica. Six Special Places. Albert Whitman,
1975.
Stop reading at "... Norma Smiled. She had an idea. "

Felder, Eleanor. X Marks the Spot. Coward-McCann, 1972.
Fluency: How many ways is X used?
Then read the book. Any new ideas?

Hill, Donna. Mrs. Glee Was Waiting. Atheneum, 1979.
Fluency: List all the reasons you can think of to
avoid doing something you don't want to
do.
List all the consequences of not doing
what you are supposed to do.

Kent, Jack. The Egg Book. Macmillan, 1975.
Fluency: List all the things that hatch out of an
egg.

Kent, Jack. Socks for Supper. Parents, 1978.
Evaluation: Determine an object you would like to
have most.
Originality: Devise a series of trades to obtain it.

Lapp, Eleanor. In the Morning Mist. Whitman, 1978.
Flexibility: What might you see early in the morning
in a country meadow that you would not
see later in the day?
List as many sights as you can.

Maestro, Betsy. Busy Day, A Book of Action Words. Crown,
1978.

Fluency: What action words describe your school day?
What action words describe your Saturdays?

Meddaugh, Susan. Too Short Fred. Houghton Mifflin, 1978.
Fluency: List all the advantages of being short.
List all the disadvantages of being very tall.
List all the good things you can think of about being you.

Most, Bernard. If the Dinosaurs Came Back. Harcourt, 1979.
Originality: What might you say and do if you arrived at school one morning and found a dinosaur in the schoolyard?

Raskin, Ellen. Nothing Ever Happens on My Block. Atheneum, 1966.
Fluency: List all the things that have happened on your block since the beginning of summer.

Ross, Tony. Little Red Hood: A Classic Story Bent out of Shape. Doubleday, 1979.
Elaboration: Try giving an old tale a new setting.
How would the characters' speech change?
What else would be different?

Sage, Alison. The Ogre's Banquet. Doubleday, 1978.
Fluency: List all the kinds of foods an ogre might eat.
Flexibility: How many different kinds of food can you list for an ogre's banquet?
Originality: What foods did you think of that no one else did?
Elaboration: Plan a banquet for an ogre.

Spier, Peter. Bored--Nothing to Do! Doubleday, 1978.
Fluency: How many things can you think to do at home on a rainy day?
Evaluation: Which thing would you do first? Why?

Stevenson, James. The Worst Person in the World. Greenwillow, 1978.
Flexibility: What other favorite story characters can you think of who might be able to help the "worst person in the world?"

Evaluation: Which character from your list will you choose to convince "the worst person in the world" to change his ways?

Originality: What will your character say or do?

Torgersen, Don. The Girl Who Tricked the Troll. Children s Press, 1978.

Flexibility: What other methods might Karen have used to drive the angry troll back into the forest?

Tresselt, Alvin. What Did You Leave Behind? Lothrop, Lee & Shepard, 1978.

Fluency: List all the places you have been that have special memories for you.

Evaluation: Which memories are most special? Why?

Ahlberg, Janet and Allan. The Little Worm Book. Viking, 1980.

A tongue-in-cheek take-off on the classic research paper, this small book will be most enjoyed by upper elementary, junior and senior high students. The 32 pages are divided into classic chapters. Sample titles include "You and Your Worm" and "A Short History of the Worm." Amid all the laughter, students are required to sort fact from fiction, moving as they do from worms with "two ends, a middle and no beginning who get bored" to a "Worm Intelligence Experiment." A perfect model for elaboration of non fiction topics!

(Fluency, Flexibility, Originality, Elaboration)

Armstrong, Louise. How to Turn War into Peace. Illus. by Bill Basso. Harcourt Brace Jovanovich, 1978.

"Susie is building her sand castle next to yours, you're in a potential TROUBLE SPOT. --If you yell. Move! You have a DISPUTE--Susie is your ADVERSARY!" So begins this example of the finest kind of book for gifted programs. The author has taken very difficult concepts (Invasion, Buffer Zone, Deterrent, Allies, Strategy, Tactics, Neutral Observers and Negotiated Settlement) and reduced them to their simplest and most easily understandable form. This is a feat in itself but with the addition of humorous illustrations the book becomes a primer on war for readers of all ages.

The book is a perfect model for students to study and enjoy before developing their own concept clusters.

(Originality, Elaboration)

Benjamin, Alan. **1000 Inventions.** Illus. by Sal Murdocca.
    Four Winds Press, 1980.
        Here are 1000 new inventions that will make even the
most veteran patent inspector sit up and take notice! How
about a "great gadget" that "helps with your homework and
eats your spinach"? Or a "wonderful whatnot" that "protects
you from monsters and does magic tricks"? And 998 more!
From the creators of the best-selling 1000 Monsters and 1000
Space Monsters (Have Landed), this is another wacky, fun-
filled flip book, with ten fabulous machines die-cut into three
parts--beginning/middle/end--and with a zany text to match.
The reader can mix-and-match to produce a full 1000 new
machines that even Rube Goldberg never dreamed of.
                                                    (Flexibility, Originality)

Charlip, Remy. **Fortunately.** Parents, 1964. Reissued by
    Four Winds, 1980.
        Fortunately Ned was invited to a surprise party. Un-
fortunately the party was a thousand miles away. Fortunately
he borrowed an airplane. Unfortunately the motor exploded....
Good fortune follows bad fortune through an exciting and hilarious series of cliffhanging escapades which lead finally to
a fortunate ending.
        This imaginative approach to the elaboration of two
simple concepts will have young readers constructing their
own "fortunately and unfortunately" adventures. Young children may need help in discovering how the author deftly
integrates the element of conflict into the story. Otherwise,
creative writing experiences may lead to a series of repetitive
phrases without resolution.   (Elaboration)

DePaola, Tomie. **The Quicksand Book.** Holiday House, 1977.
        Poor jungle girl! She falls into the quicksand. Jungle
boy finds her. Jungle Girl starts to sink while Jungle Boy
tells her: (1) Where and how quicksand forms; (2) Why people sink in quicksand; (3) What happens to animals in quicksand; (4) How people can watch out for quicksand; (5) What
people should do if they fall into quicksand.
        But Jungle Girl does not sink forever. In a happy and
surprise ending she is both the rescued and the rescuer.
        This is a delightful example of incorporating basic facts
within a funny story. It can serve as an excellent model for
gifted students who have researched basic information and are
ready to elaborate on it for a presentation.   (Elaboration)

Jarrell, Randall. A Bat Is Born. Illus. by John Schoenherr.
　　Doubleday, 1978.
　　　　"A bat is born
　　　　Naked and blind and pale
　　　　His mother makes a pocket of her tail
　　　　And catches him. "
　　So begins A Bat Is Born, the beautiful poem by Randall Jarrell from his novel, The Bat-Poet. In lovely cadences
the poet describes the graceful existence of a common brown
bat caring for her young. Illustrations and poetry blend to
create the bat's haunting grace and demonstrate a unique descriptive approach to a topic normally discussed in dry, factual terms. A Bat Is Born is a beautiful model for students
to use in elaborating on a non-fiction topic.
　　　　　　　　　　　　　(Elaboration, Description)

Oakley, Graham. Magical Changes. Atheneum, 1979.
　　This beautiful and unusual book is a visual tour to
which the viewer will return again and again. Young mathe-
maticians may be challenged to discover how many unique
combinations the illustrator has created as they turn the half-
pages, all of which match, no matter what the turn!
　　Peaceful swans sailing on a stream? No indeed: swan
bodies holding up a railroad bridge--or is it swan bodies that
are really candles, or are they even the bottoms of ancient
Greek statues? Who can tell for sure, because magical
changes make it all possible.
　　The gentlemen holding umbrellas on one page are supporting dead tree trunks alive with spider webs on another,
or carrying a wedding cake on still another. All of the
images are the product of the illustrator's fabulous imagination and his skill in creating an amazing diversity of pictures
which mix and match in surprising ways. A perfect example
of flexibility of thinking in action!
　　　　　　　　(Flexibility, Originality, Visual Literacy)

Prelutsky, Jack. Rolling Harvey Down the Hill. Illus. by
　　Victoria Chess. Morrow, 1980.
　　Here is a collection of poetry sure to rival Silverstein's Where the Sidewalk Ends for humor and originality.
The poems describe the antics and escapades of a less-than-
charming gang of children, Lumpy, Tony, Willie, Harvey and
the narrator. They live in an apartment house but their environment does not prove restricting in the least. Eyebrows
may be raised at some of the antics but children will enjoy

the flow of the language and the fresh, original approach.
(Originality)

Rockwell, Thomas. The Portmanteau Book. Little, Brown
& Co. , 1974.
    While not a picture book in the truest sense, this
heavily illustrated book for older readers is a perfect blend
of fluent, flexible and original thought and a must for gifted
programs.
    The Portmanteau Book is a collection of plays, short
stories, poems, recipes, crossword puzzles, games, comic
books, and much, much more. It contains charming, witty
poems; a story in which not only every word and line is
written backwards, but it starts at the end and ends at the
beginning; and another story (among many) called "Naked-
ness, " in which a boy totally humiliates his brother by yelling
fire while his brother is taking a bath. Also included are
nonsensical recipes for "Fruit Kiss, " "Liver Punishment, "
and "Fried Hall Closet. " It closes with a humorous poll con-
cerning the popularity of the book. Young writers will find a
wide variety of "off beat" ideas here!
(Fluency, Flexibility, Originality)

Ross, Dave. A Book of Hugs. Illus. by the author. Thomas
Y. Crowell, 1979.
    Never before has the hug--that simple gesture of af-
fection--been so carefully scrutinized, analyzed, classified,
and explained. Here are hugs of every kind, briefly defined
and humorously pictured: animal hugs (like the fish hug--
warning: never hug a shark!); people hugs (like the Great
Aunt Mary hug--leaves you with lipstick on your cheek); thing
hugs (blankets); and special hugs (birthdays).
    The publisher explains that author Ross spent years
compiling this collection of embraces. What body language
research and interpretation might students do? A book of
smiles, frowns, hands, shrugs, nods??
(Fluency, Flexibility, Originality, Elaboration)

Scarry, Huck. On Wheels. Illus. in four colors by the author. Philomel Books, 1980.
    From when the cavemen first discovered wheels,
through chariots, horse-drawn carriages, steam-powered wag-
ons, and up to snappy roadsters, time-traveler Peter Pebble
takes readers on a spirited tour of wheels throughout the cen-

turies. Richly detailed, carefully researched drawings and a very simple text make this an engaging introduction to the history of wheeled vehicles and machines and a mind-expanding adventure for young readers. As a visual experience alone, children should be encouraged to note the changes in the evolution of the wheel. As an experience in fluent and flexible thinking, how many wheels can students discover which are not included in the book? How many uses of wheels can students name? (Fluency, Flexibility)

Schwartz, Alvin. Kickle Snifters and Other Fearsome Critters. Illus. by Glen Rounds. Lippincott, 1976.
Here you will meet an amazing collection of creatures of the mind, tall-tale imaginary creations of "frontiersmen, woodsmen, cowboys, and carnival sharps to prank the tenderfoot and pass the time." This is a collection of one-of-a-kind characters to challenge students' imaginations and get creative juices flowing.

Meet the tripodero with its elevator-like motion, stretching to enormous heights to hunt. Meet too, the lufferlang, so grotesque it frightens itself; or the goofus bird, which flies backward to see where it has been.

This original and imaginative work is complete with "notes" and a tongue-in-cheek bibliography. (Originality)

Chapter 5

BOOKS TO FOSTER CRITICAL THINKING

"The whole art of teaching is only the art of awakening the natural curiosity of young minds for the purpose of satisfying them afterwards."

Gifted children often demonstrate greater ability than their peers to hold many ideas at once, along with the ability to compare more ideas with one another. They look at the world a bit differently, easily handling analytical and factual concepts while at the same time finding satisfaction in the world of fantasy and imagination. They are sharp observers of a more complex universe, and have a broad awareness of self including a high degree of self-criticism.

The gifted child is, in fact, a paradox who has been described as both more primitive and more cultured, more destructive and more constructive, crazier and saner than the average person.

Programs for the gifted most often center on nurturing intelligence, mental brightness, the capacity to generalize, to conceptualize, to reason abstractly and to solve problems. Yet, if one understands the capacity of the gifted child to operate comfortably in both cognitive and affective areas, every effort should be made to provide experiences which focus on both areas.

There is no greater magic than that which evolves from reality and life itself. School libraries are brimming with books which can reawaken or confirm that awe and mystery which surrounds all living things. A sense of wonder is inherent in children and books can help to nourish that appreciation of beauty-from a grass blade to a star; can help to keep alive that reverence for life and its infinite variation. (from E Is for Everybody)

Fine picture books are among the most valuable resources available to the teacher of gifted, for through them
the children can know both real and fanciful worlds and discover that basic truths are to be found in each. In developing
critical thinking skills it matters not if the book is fact or
fantasy as long as it helps children to listen more acutely,
look more intently and touch more genuinely the literary world
created for them.

Critical Thinking Skills

The child who is able to think critically senses when
problems exist and can rearrange thought processes to deal
with them. This child recognizes discontinuities and incon-
sistencies and can work with concentration to redefine the
elements of a task. In addition, the gifted child's ability to
be fluent and flexible in thinking patterns enables him or her
to support or deny initial guesses and hypotheses and to form
new ones with relative ease.

In working with children in critical thinking areas it
is important to stress open-mindedness; the need for gathering
additional information before drawing conclusions; the need to
question and to avoid common mistakes in reasoning, and to
separate emotional from logical thinking.

To nurture these abilities four critical thinking areas
come into play: planning, forecasting, decision-making, and
problem solving. Each area can be successfully explored
through picture books.

Planning concerns the development of a series of steps
to achieve a specific solution or outcome. Activities in planning can be undertaken by even the very youngest to encourage
involvement in learning and the development of responsibility.

In Lorna Balian's Sometimes It's Turkey, Sometimes
It's Feathers (Abingdon, 1975) Mrs. Gumm finds a turkey
egg in the woods and immediately begins planning her Thanksgiving dinner which is several months away. She carefully
follows all the steps in the planning process:

1) She identifies what she wants to do (Hatch the egg
   and raise the turkey)
2) Identifies the materials she will need (Food and
   shelter for the turkey)

"He'll be bigger—and much plumper—next Thanksgiving,"
said little old Mrs. Gumm.
"IMAGINE!"

3) Considers the steps to be taken (Hatch the egg, fatten the turkey, make preparations for the Thanksgiving dinner, including preparing the hatchet for the turkey's end)
4) Seeks to identify the problems which might be encountered (Here is where Mrs. Gumm's planning process falls down).

In sharing this delightful book as an introduction to the planning process, children will quickly see that failure to anticipate problems which might arise can ruin the best made plans. Mrs. Gumm, of course, failed to anticipate the problem of her growing attachment to the turkey!

Forecasting is related to planning but goes beyond the planning process to examine causes and effects and to predict probable outcomes.

In The King's Monster by Carolyn Haywood (Morrow, 1980) the childhood sweetheart of the princess can win her hand only if he overcomes the king's monster who dwells in the dungeon of the palace. The princess is determined to accompany him.

Note how following the steps in the forecasting procedure can add to the excitement of the story, while at the same time fostering the skill of forecasting.

1) Consider all the possible causes and effects of the situation.

Causes	Effects
Why is there a monster in the dungeon? Who put it there? What does it do to cause fear in everyone?	What will happen if they do find the monster? What will happen if they don't find the monster?

2) Look at the quality of each cause and effect related to the situation.
3) Choose the best cause and/or effect.

Will the class decide to confront the monster or run away? This will depend on their ability to forecast with the facts at hand. As students examine the quality of each of their predictions they must develop reasons for the choices they make.

Decision-Making is the process of making informed choices regarding the situation or problem to be resolved. The decision-making procedure is one of examining a number of alternatives in order to arrive at a single judgment.

While numerous picture books present decision-making opportunities for their protagonists, the folk or fairy tale is ideal for stimulating thinking about choices. In his Uses of Enchantment, Bruno Bettelheim says:

> The fairy tale confronts the child squarely with the basic human predicaments.... [It] states an essential dilemma [and] permits the child to come to grips with the problem in its most essential form ... from them [fairy tales] the child can learn more about the inner problems of man, and about solutions to his own predicaments in society than he can from any other type story within his comprehension.

The decision-making process involves:

1) Thinking of many alternatives to a problem one wishes to solve.
2) Establishing criteria for weighing each alternative.
3) Weighing the alternatives in terms of the criteria.
4) Eliminating alternatives and narrowing to a single judgment, choice or decision.
5) Supporting or defining the decision by giving several reasons for the choice.

In Elizabeth Winthrop's Journey to the Bright Kingdom (Holiday House, 1979) Kiyo discovers a magical underground kingdom ruled by mice where there is no sadness, sickness or blindness. She longs to take her blind and dying mother to the kingdom so that she can see again at least for a time. Kiyo's father forbids even the thought of such a journey; he fears for his wife's life and is convinced that such a place cannot exist. Kiyo knows that blindness has left her mother with no will to live. The decision she must make is as difficult for Kiyo as it will be for the young reader.

Problem Solving

Creative problem solving, whatever is used, encourages the development of an open mind and calls upon all of the productive and critical thinking skills. Both fluency and flexibility of thought are essential in seeking and testing solutions. Planning, forecasting and decision-making skills are often employed as well as creative and original thought.

Problem-solving models can be found in most gifted programs and can be used by children in predicting how characters in literature might overcome obstacles and solve problems. In using picture books as problem-solving vehicles teachers often discover that the solutions arrived at by children are sometimes more logical (and at the same time more creative) than the author's.

The problem-solving process that follows is an elaboration of the basic problem presented in Chris Van Allsburg's The Garden of Abdul Gasazi (Houghton Mifflin, 1979).

OFF LIMITS!

Just at the edge of the town where you live lies the estate of an eccentric recluse. The grounds and buildings are surrounded by stone and iron fences and the gate to the estate is always locked. A boldly lettered sign on the gate reads: ABSOLUTELY NO ONE ALLOWED INSIDE THESE GATES: KEEP OUT: NOT RESPONSIBLE FOR WHATEVER MAY HAPPEN TO PEOPLE OR ANIMALS WHO IGNORE THIS WARNING!!!

You are riding your bike on a warm summer afternoon with your dog, Sam, running along beside you. Sam spots a rabbit and chases it to the edge of the estate. THE GATES ARE WIDE OPEN! Sam and the rabbit disappear inside the forbidden estate grounds. What will you do?

After you have worked out this problem to your satisfaction, using the questions to help you, you may want to see how others have solved problems similar to this one. Read: The Garden of Abdul Gasazi by Chris Van Allsburg (Houghton Mifflin, 1979).

To solve this problem, try the following steps:

I. State the facts leading to the problem: (WHO is involved? WHAT are the circumstances? WHEN did it happen? WHY did it happen?)

    _____

    _____

II. What is the actual problem? Can you state the problem in more than one way?

    _____

    _____

III. List as many solutions as you can to the problem. Do
      not evaluate the solutions, simply list as many as you
      can think of.

    1. _____

    2. _____

    3. _____

    4. _____

    5. _____

IV. Select two of the above solutions you think might work
     best. Tell what would probably happen as a result of
     each of these solutions.

    Solution # _____ _____

    _____

    Solution # _____ _____

    _____

V.   Which solution will you choose? Why? _____

    _____

Summary: The following step-by-step summaries of critical
          thinking processes were developed by Joyce Juntune,
          Executive Director of the National Association for Gifted
          Children, and are included here with her permission.

Planning

The Planning Process includes the following steps:

1. Identification: Stating what you want to do (problem or
    project) with enough additional information to explain what
    you plan to accomplish. For example:
    What do you want to do?
    What else can you tell about your idea to make it
    clearer?

2. <u>Materials:</u>   List the materials necessary to carry out the project.

3. <u>Steps:</u>   List the steps involved in actually carrying out the plan.   Organization of materials, time, resources must be provided for.   For example:
    > Where are all the things you will have to do to complete your plan?
    > Which is first, second, etc.?
    > Mark each step with a time showing when should be completed.
    > NOTE: It is wise to encourage the student to include gathering materials as the first step and putting materials away as the last step.

4. <u>Problems:</u>   Considering problems one might encounter in carrying out the plan.
    For example:
    > What problems might you have in carrying out your plan?
    > Will you have any problems with your materials?
    > Think of as many different kinds of problems as you can.

Forecasting

The forecasting process includes the following steps (It is not always necessary to have the students do all the steps but they should have the knowledge of what comes before and after the step they are working with):

1. Consider all the possible causes and results for a given situation.
    For example:
    > List several causes and effects of the following situation ....
    > Think of many possible causes and effects of ....

2. The student examines the quality of each of the causes or effects related to the given situation.
    For example:
    > Mark the strongest cause and effect with a +.
    > Mark the weakest cause and effect with a -.

3. Choose the best cause and/or effect.
    For example:

Examine all the + causes and effects.   Choose the one you think is the strongest.

4.   Give reasons to support your choice.

Decision-Making

Decision-making follows the following steps:

1.   Alternatives: the teacher encourages the student to think of many alternatives to a problem he/she wished to solve.

2.   Criteria: the teacher assists the student in establishing criteria for weighing each alternative.

3.   Weighing: the teacher assists the student in weighing his/her alternatives in terms of his/her criteria.   The following grid may be used for this purpose.

Alternative
Alternative
Alternative
Alternative

4.   Judgment: the teacher guides the student in eliminating some of the alternatives and encourages him/her to make a single judgment, choice or decision.
   a.   The top choice on the criteria chart is not necessarily the best judgment.
   b.   There may be several choices which rank very close together.
   c.   The student may want to develop a solution for a low criterion as a specific alternative.
   d.   The student may want to weigh his/her criteria.
   e.   The student may wish to add other criteria to support his/her choice of an alternative.   This is pushing for flexibility.

5.   Reasons: the teacher encourages the student to support or defend his/her decision by giving reasons for his/her choice.

a. It is important to allow students to share their ideas
    and results. There is pleasure in delving into other
    people's thoughts and ideas and learning goes hand in
    hand with pleasure.

6. Sample warm-ups:
    a. "If you could only eat one kind of food for a whole
        week, what would you eat? Think of at least five
        alternatives (choices). While you're thinking about
        your decision, consider these criteria:
        (1) Do I like it?
        (2) Will it be good for me?
        (3) Can I afford it?
        (4) Will my parents let me?
        (5) Will I get tired of it?
    Carefully make your choice. Give reasons for your choice. "
    b. "We have read many interesting stories. Which one
        do you think is the best? Think of three stories that
        you like. (These are your alternatives.) Consider
        the following criteria as you make your choice:
        (1) Does it have a good ending?
        (2) Did it keep me interested?
        (3) Would I recommend it to a friend?
    Give three reasons for your choice. "

Problem Solving--One Approach

Summary of steps in the problem-solving process:

1. State the problem in two or three different ways.

2. State factors which contribute to the problem (who, what,
    when, where, why).

3. State the criteria the solution must meet.

4. Brainstorm all possible solutions:
    a) Every answer is acceptable at this point.
    b) Children are encouraged to hitch-hike on each other's
        answers.
    c) The best solutions may well occur in the last 25%
        of the responses.

5. Compare solutions with criteria listed in step three.

6. Choose the solution which best meets the criteria.

The titles which follow have been selected for their usefulness in fostering critical thinking skills. Again, it is difficult to categorize an excellent picture book, for the best can be used in many ways. However, for ease of selection in working with a particular skill, an attempt has been made to categorize titles in those areas where they have been successfully used with boys and girls.

Alexander, Lloyd. The King's Fountain. Illus. by Ezra Jack Keats. E. P. Dutton, 1971.

The king has decided to build a huge and beautiful fountain in his garden. If he does, the town below will not get any water and the people will all be thirsty. A poor man in the city realizes this and he goes to the wise man, the glib merchants and the strongest man in the village to get them to go to the King and stop the building of the fountain. But none of them will go. Only one man realizes the danger and can do the task--the poor man himself. What will the reader predict at this point in the story? Can the poor man face the King and be wise, glib, and strong and brave? The story shows man's ability to act and call upon his resources when the situation demands his action. (Forecasting)

Alexander, Lloyd. The Truthful Harp. Illus. by Evaline Ness. Holt, 1967.

Have you ever heard of a king who didn't want to be king? Well, Fflewddur Flam, the delightful king of a kingdom "he could stride across between mid-day and noon," didn't want to be king. He wanted to be a bard and play the harp. So he practiced and practiced and then went to the Chief Bard to get permission to become a Bard. But once there he forgot all he knew and flunked the test. Poor Fflewddur! The Chief Bard took pity on him and gave him a magic harp that even he could make play beautiful music. Fflewddur set out on the road to be a Bard. His adventures with this wonderful harp and the lessons he learned about himself are all revealed when he returns to the Hall of the Chief Bard. There he learns the true worth of his misadventures and finds out something very important about himself.

Young readers who understand that the harp is a visible symbol of Fflewddur's conscience will have no problem with the hapless King's decision to carry the harp with him always. Students, however, who read on a literal level will need help in understanding the decision. (Decision-making)

Alexander, Sue. Whatever Happened to Uncle Albert? And

Other Puzzling Plays. Illus. by Tom Huffman. Houghton Mifflin/Clarion Books, 1980.
    While this is a slight step up from the picture book
format, gifted children on the primary level will delight in
solving these mysteries before the author does. The four
short original plays are different in tone. There is a Sherlock Holmes-style mystery, a werewolf transformation play,
a contemporary slapstick mystery, and a play involving a
trial. Each presents a problem for the young detective to
solve and each can be presented using a minimum of props
and costumes.   (Problem solving)

Balian, Lorna. Sometimes It's Turkey, Sometimes It's
    Feathers. Abingdon, 1975.
    Mrs. Gumm finds a turkey egg in the woods. She
takes the egg home and vows to Cat that they will take expert care of the egg in hopes that it will hatch. Then they
will have a fine turkey to feast upon by Thanksgiving Day.
After a long wait the egg does hatch in May. Little old Mrs.
Gumm and Cat have all summer to fatten Turkey up and also
to become very attached to him. That's just what they did.
Turkey ate everything! Turkey ate all Mrs. Gumm gave him
and much much more. He ate the strawberries, garden seed,
raspberries, grapes and the catfood. November rolled around
and Mrs. Gumm made all the necessary preparations for their
Thanksgiving dinner--not the least being to prepare the hatchet
for Turkey's end. At last it was time to eat. Mrs. Gumm
had the table set and left to bring the nice plump turkey back.
That's just what she did. The surprise? Mrs. Gumm led
Turkey to his place at the table and sat down to dine with her
two fine friends, Cat and Turkey. Of course, Turkey will
be much bigger by next year and Mrs. Gumm will have to begin her planning all over again!   (Planning)

Boedecker, N. M. The Mushroom Center Disaster. Illus. by
    Erik Blegvad. Atheneum, 1974.
    In a tiny fantasy village deep in a woodland clearing
a group of ladybugs, beetles and crickets live happily in a
mushroom village. Disaster strikes one night when careless
campers dump their trash on top of the village, totally destroying it. The next morning the survivors survey the ruins
with dismay. Their homes, yards and gardens have been
crushed beyond repair by a wide variety of rubbish. Instead
of leaving the village, however, the inhabitants work together
to rebuild it, using all of the items of rubbish.
    This is a perfect vehicle for introducing the planning
process. Challenge students to find useful purposes for the

following items in rebuilding the miniature village: one large soda bottle, three transparent candy wrappers, numerous pieces of tinfoil, a large chunk of chewing gum (chewed), two tin cans, one aluminum pie-pan with holes in the bottom, six straws and a number of cigarette butts. Encourage students to look beyond their first ideas to develop a use for each in an overall plan of reconstruction.

(Planning, Fluency, Flexibility)

Boedecker, N. M. Quimble Wood. Illus. by the author. Atheneum, 1981.

There were once four quimbles in a box: Quilliam, Quilice, Quint and the unstoppable Quenelope, each no bigger than your little finger. When their box fell out of a car on a forest road the Quimbles had to fend for themselves. Winter was near. There were food and firewood to gather, a house to build, winter clothes, furniture, pots and pans to improvise. In fact, the reader will plan right along with the Quimbles as to how to make the best use of the available resources in order to survive!

After a near disaster with fire, and just when the ice has begun to form at the edge of the pond each night, their new home at last is ready and well-stocked for winter. Here is a delightfully fresh approach to "making do" to challenge young readers and thinkers! (Planning)

Bolliger, Max. The Wooden Man. Illus. by Fred Bauer. The Seabury Press, 1974.

Close to a wheat field live seven birds: the father bird, the mother bird and their five children. The birds are so happy with their lives that every evening they sing together in the top of a pear tree. And every morning they greet the new day with a song.

"How beautiful," say the sun, the wind and the rain.

Then one day a wooden man appears in the middle of the wheat field. In his hand the wooden man holds a gun, and four or five times a day he shoots it into the air. The great noise frightens the birds. They hide in the woods and stop singing. The sun, the wind and the rain see what was happening. "Who is this man?", they ask.

"He has no eyes", says the sun.

"He has no ears", says the wind.

"He has no heart", says the rain.

So they decide to join forces against him.

In this book the author sets up a tantalizing problem for readers of all ages to contemplate. Readers who see this as a satire on modern society may or may not agree with the ultimate resolution!   (Problem solving)

Bowden, Joan Chase. Why the Tides Ebb and Flow. Illus.
    by Marc Brown. Houghton Mifflin Company, 1979.
        Twice every day the sea laps up and covers the shore.
And twice each day it flows out over the shining sand. All
this would never have come to be if the Sky Spirit had taken
a moment to think. But he didn't and because of that the
stubborn old woman tricks him.
        Old woman has no hut. One morning she goes to the
Sky Spirit and asks for one, but he is far too busy. So she
bides her time and asks again, this time for only a rock to
shelter her. "Take one," he answers carelessly.
        This is just what the stubborn old woman wanted to
hear. Gleefully she climbs into her stewpot and sets sail on
the great green ocean. And this is the story that tells how
she came by someone who would love and protect her, someone who would keep her company, someone who would build
her a hut--and why the tides ebb and flow.
        Wanting something in a busy world, whether from Sky
Spirits or preoccupied parents, is a familiar situation that
calls for considerable planning. The reader will enjoy the
strategy the old woman employs to get what she wants and
will perhaps realize that planning is the first step to success!
                                              (Planning)

Bowen, Gary. A Special Gift for Mother. Wood engravings
    designed by Gary Bowen and engraved by Randy Miller.
    Farrar, Straus and Giroux, 1980.
        The creators of My Village, Sturbridge take us on an-
other excursion into early-nineteenth-century New England.
This time we follow Pliny Freeman, the village cooper's son,
as he goes about making sufficient goods to trade at Mr.
Knight's store for a special gift for Mother: an imported red
and white china coffeepot, priced at $1. 37.
        Today's young people will be fascinated by Pliny's re-
sourcefulness. He carves two gross of wooden clothespins
and a batch of hoe handles, braids broad-brimmed straw hats
and rawhide oxen whips, sets a trap for mink and barters
hours of cranking a lathe for five maple rolling pins. Through
much planning, swapping and work Pliny does meet his goal
and obtains the special gift for Mother.
        After sharing this title, talk with students about a
seemingly impossible goal each might have. Can students
map out a reasonable plan to reach their individual goals?
                                              (Planning)

Carrick, Carol. The Climb. Illus. by Donald Carrick.
    Houghton Mifflin/Clarion Books, 1980.
    "I'm scared, " Brendan
says as his older cousin, Nora,
coaxes him to climb the mountain.
    "What a baby, " thinks
Nora.
    After Brendan, with her
help, finally makes it to the top
and begins to gather confidence,
Nora decides to play a trick on
him.   Trying not to laugh out
loud, she growls like a bear.
Her trick backfires, though,
when she gets stuck in the cave.
Will Brendan use the opportunity to get even with Nora for
her tricks?   Children will debate his decision!
                              (Decision-making)

Cooper, Susan. Jethro and the Jumbie. Illus. by Ashley
    Bryan. Atheneum, 1979.
    Jethro has turned into a bag of bad temper. He will
be eight next week and his big brother has promised to take
him deep sea fishing when he is that old. Now Thomas says
he is too small to go! Jethro stomps away up the hill,
though the trail is supposed to be haunted by the spirits of
the dead called jumbies. He doesn't care. He really doesn't
believe in jumbies.
    But meet one he does--and though he is scared he is
still too mad to believe in that jumbie. The poor jumbie
grows dimmer and smaller until Jethro strikes a bargain with
him. If the jumbie will make brother Thomas keep his promise, Jethro will believe in him. What will happen when Jethro
and the jumbie return to the town to find Thomas? Predicting
the outcome of this funny, warmhearted tale can be a real
challenge for young thinkers. The vocabulary is highly descriptive and the illustrations sensitively executed.
                              (Forecasting)

Dos Santos, Joyce Audy. The Diviner. Illus. by the author.
    Lippincott, 1980.
    Here is a tale of the life of one who supposedly can
foretell the future, and the trouble in which this can land him!
Lucky, lazy Jean-Pierre predicts that the miller's wife will

have a son. He advises a shepherd whose flock has been carried off by a wolf that the beast will not return. Such shrewd guesswork earns him the reputation of being a diviner. And a diviner is just what the king needs to find the Queen's missing ring. The fact that he has no idea where the ring might be doesn't bother Jean-Pierre in the least.... Students will delight in predicting the ending to this tale!

(Forecasting)

Galdone, Joanna. The Little Girl and the Big Bear. Illus.
    by Paul Galdone. Houghton Mifflin/Clarion Books,
    1980.
    Once long ago a Little Girl lost her way in the woods while picking berries. Just before dark, she came upon a deserted hut where she decided to spend the night. Suddenly, the Little Girl heard a great roar and in walked a huge Bear.

The Bear turned the Little Girl into his servant and told her she could never go home again. But the Little Girl was cleverer than the Bear. She thought of an ingenious way to make him take her back to her grandparents.

Here is a problem with a twist. Note that children are challenged to think of ways not to escape the Bear, but to force the Bear to return the child. As children work toward unique solutions to the problem they should follow basic problem-solving steps. First, define the problem. Second, brainstorm for solutions. Third, set criteria for a successful solution, and fourth, examine their solutions in light of the criteria set. Children may well discover that their solutions are better than the author's! (Problem solving)

Giblin, James and Dale Ferguson. The Scarecrow Book. Crown, 1980.

How does one deter birds that destroy crops? Here is problem solving and fluency of thought in action. The authors have described and illustrated with photographs man's battle with harmful birds through the centuries and the creative measures taken to deal with the problem. From placing guards on the fields to playing tapes of frightened birds, to the time-honored scarecrow, the book is a chronicle of man's ingenuity. Included are scarecrows from many times and places, along with directions for making a scarecrow. Here is a real opportunity for creative self-expression in a problem-solving situation. (Problem solving)

Gill, Bob. A Balloon for a Blunderbuss. Illus. by Alastair Reid. Harper & Row, 1961.

A treasure of a captured butterfly begins a flight of fantasy as the owner imagines what he might get in trade for his prized catch. His imagination totally captivates him as he begins a mind-boggling swap-shop. He trades for a variety of things from a wishbone to a blunderbuss. Each trade is bigger and better until he becomes the owner of his own army and then an island.

He marvels at the fact that it all began with a butterfly and he is now the owner of everything. He opens his cupped hands to show his butterfly and in a soundless second the prized catch is free and his captor must return to reality-- as must the reader in this exercise in decision-making.

Haywood, Carolyn. The King's Monster. Illus. by Victor Ambrus. Morrow, 1980.

The king laughs whenever his subjects complain about the dreadful and dangerous beast that lurks in his dungeon. But when his beautiful daughter, Gabriella, is sixteen and the palace is besieged by her suitors, the situation grows more serious. Then he announces that only the man who can overcome the monster can win his daughter's hand. Together, Gabriella and Prince Michael, her childhood sweetheart, descend into the deepest dungeon. What will they meet? What fears will they face before they can deal with them? Students will enjoy predicting the unusual outcome of this cheerful fairy tale of true love and courage rewarded. (Forecasting)

Hill, Eric. Where's Spot? Illus. by the author. G. P. Putnam's Sons, 1980.
Perfect for forecasting, this is a "lift up the flap and find a surprise" book for the very young. Where's Spot features a mother dog looking for her puppy, Spot. Each page asks a question: Is he behind the door? Is he inside the clock? Is he in the piano?
Hiding under each flap is a different animal saying, "No!" There's a honey bear behind the door, a friendly alligator under the bed, a monkey in the closet. And imagine lifting up the top of a grand piano and finding a hippopotamus smiling sweetly.
Spot, of course, is where every good puppy should be, in his basket. But his mother looks in eight different places, giving young viewers eight guesses before she finds him.
(Forecasting)

Jacques, Faith. Tilly's House. Illus. by the author. Atheneum, 1979.
The book begins with, "Upstairs in the doll house lived a family of wooden dolls." Father worked in his study, mother sewed in the parlor, children played in the nursery and Tilly, the kitchenmaid did all the work. She was a wooden Cinderella working from daylight to dusk. Tilly didn't mind the work but she resented being ordered around and always pushed to do more.
One night she decides that things will never change and she must be free to decide things for herself. Her independent nature encourages her to pack her bag, get her knitting and sewing box, pick up her umbrella and tiptoe out the door.
Tilly leaves the doll house for the big world and discovers it is indeed a big world. She meets Edward the teddy bear who agrees to help her find a home of her own. Tilly

rejects the idea of living in the big house, as it still would
not be a home of her own.

Edward takes her to a deserted greenhouse. Tilly
sees great possibilities for an old wooden box and believes
she has at last found her place. The little wooden doll transforms the box into an immaculate little house of her own.
Tilly is a study in determination, ingenuity and the rewards
of hard work, all concepts the gifted child must think deeply
about.

The book can serve as an excellent tool for forecasting
activities. Read aloud to the point where Tilly tiptoes out the
door. What will students predict for Tilly's future?

Kraus, Robert and Kraus, Bruce. The Detective of London.
Illus. by Robert Byrd. Windmill Books, 1977.

The Detective of London is confronted by his most
baffling case when the recently unearthed dinosaur bones disappear from the London Docks.

Noted artist Robert Byrd recreates Victorian London
from the Halls of Parliament down to the last miniature gas-
light as the Detective takes us on a tour throughout the under-
world of London. He searches for clues, witnesses and in-
formants and eats his way from Trafalgar Square to Piccadilly
Circus. Can young readers unearth the culprit and find the
bones before the Detective does? Keen powers of deduction
are needed for this Sherlock Holmes spoof!

(Problem solving, Forecasting)

Kroll, Steven. Amanda and the Giggling Ghost. Illus. by
Dick Gaskenback. Holiday House, 1980.

One night, Amanda's hairbrush falls off the bureau with
a loud bang. Then her jewelry box crashes against the wall
and her paint set clatters to the floor. A giggling ghost is
flying around Amanda's room--and stealing her things!

Amanda chases the ghost out of the door and through
the town. Before she can stop him, he steals a baseball
glove, a chicken, three tubes of toothpaste and numerous other
items. Soon the whole town is in a uproar. No one believes
Amanda when she says the ghost is the thief. How can Amanda stop a ghost from stealing and regain her credibility in the
eyes of the town. Problem solvers, unite! (Problem solving)

Lorenz, Lee. Scornful Simkin. Illus. by the author.
Prentice-Hall, 1980.

Here, for the first time as a picture book, is Chaucer's "The Reeve's Tale," in a retelling that captures all the richness and roguery of the original. Scornful Simkin, the terrible-tempered miller who grinds other people's grain, but always keeps a little for himself, matches wits with Alan and John, two high-spirited students from Cambridge University who attempt to beat the miller at his own game. Even the youngest listener will have ample opportunity for forecasting the outcome of numerous instances of trickery and deception, adventure and misadventure. This is an excellent introduction to Chaucer for older readers, and a delightful tale for younger children.   (Forecasting)

Low, Joseph.   What If....?   Illus. by the author.   Atheneum, 1976.
   What If....? is a forecaster's delight! The author/ illustrator lets imagination run wild as he dreams up divergent situations which call for a variety of solutions. There are fourteen "what ifs" in the book, ranging from what one might do if asked to go swimming with a shark to what to do if an elephant sits down on your seesaw. Children will delight in resolving the problems presented here!
                                                       (Forecasting)

McDermott, Gerald.   Papagayo, The Mischief Maker.   Illus. by the author.   Windmill-Wanderer Books, 1980.
   Crawk! Papagayo the parrot soars through the rosy sky and greets the bright new morning. Laughing and squawking, he calls to all to join in his fun. But his raucous cries disturb the night creatures' day-time sleep, and they will have none of his mischief. Instead, they huddle in the leafy green shadows and hide. It isn't until the truly frightening moon-dog comes to gobble up their beloved moon that the night creatures come to appreciate the talents of Papagayo.
   Very young listeners will delight in predicting just how Papagayo will use his talents to keep the moon from being destroyed. The vivid illustrations are a visual tour and capture the flavor of the Amazon as well as the art of its people.
                                                       (Forecasting)

McGovern, Ann.   Half A Kingdom.   Illus. by Nola Langner. Frederick Warne, 1977.
   One fine morning, when Prince Lini rides into the forest, he is swept away by a mysterious fog. The distressed

king offers half a kingdom for whoever can find and return
his son. The strongest and wisest men in the kingdom search
far and wide, to no avail.

But when Signy, the peasant girl, hears of the missing
prince and all those looking "far and wide" for him, she sets
out on the quest as well. "I'll look near and narrow," she
thought. Wise to the ways of the forest, Signy finds the prince
asleep in a cave, discovering that he has been captured and
imprisoned by trolls.

Signy does free the prince, using only those gifts she
possesses--her knowledge of the woods and her keen powers
of observation. How she accomplishes this will make an interesting problem-solving situation for the reader to explore.

(Problem solving)

McPhail, David. Grandfather's Cake. Charles Scribner's
    Sons, 1979.

If you think taking a piece of fresh, warm chocolate
cake to your grandfather should be an easy thing to do, maybe
you're forgetting just how good a piece of warm chocolate cake
can smell.

Travel along with Peter, Andrew and their pony,
Peaches, as they set out to deliver Grandfather's cake and
see just how difficult it can be to protect this delicious mor-
sel! Saving the cake from the fox and the bear is difficult
enough, but how can two small boys and a donkey rescue the
cake from a tall masked robber? There are many opportunities here to predict as well as outcomes to enjoy.

(Forecasting)

Mayer, Mercer. Mrs. Beggs and the Wizard. Parents,
    1973.

Mrs. Beggs' boarding house is visited by an evil wizard who does all sorts of terrible things. He turns her beautiful garden into a briar and weed patch, makes it rain on
the other guests in the parlor, flies old man Blagget in his
wheelchair across town, and causes a blizzard to rage throughout the house. Mrs. Beggs liberates the house by using
witchcraft of her own. As the guests begin to complain of
boredom, a new guest dressed in black and with a tail covered
with spines knocks at the door. One is left to imagine the
happenings the new stranger will bring. (Forecasting)

Myers, Walter Dean. The Golden Serpent. Illus. by Alice
    and Martin Provensen. Viking Press, 1980.

There are those in gifted education who feel that a book is most appropriate for a gifted child if it leaves the child with more questions than answers. This is such a book, a symbolic tale that presents a problem and then solves it ... or does it?

High on a mountain lives a wise man named Pundabi. A young boy named Ali lives with him. One day the king summons Pundabi and Ali and demands that Pundabi solve a mystery or be thrown in jail. But what is the mystery? The king does not know. Pundabi and Ali walk through the bustling market place and return to the king with the answer. It is the mystery of the Golden Serpent, which, like real life, leaves the most important questions unanswered. Be prepared for lively discussions after sharing this! (Problem solving)

Oakley, Graham. The Church Mice at Bay. Atheneum, 1978.
Everyone in Wortlethorpe, including the church mice and Sampson, the church cat, hopes the holiday curate will be a nice quiet chap like the one they had last year.

He isn't.

What's more, this trendy young curate hates mice, and considers it a church cat's duty to catch them, not to hob nob with them. Changes, changes, but the worst change of all is NO CHEESE. Plainly, something has to be done. "Eyes and ears were one thing, but a person's (or mouse's) stomach was sacred."

With fun and humor the author/artist presents a delightful problem-solving situation for the reader, with a number of options to consider. (Problem solving)

Pellowski, Anne. The Nine Crying Dolls. Illus. by Charles
Mikolaycak. Philomel Books in cooperation with the
U.S. Committee for UNICEF, 1980.
This folktale provides an authentic introduction to the cultural traditions of Poland and presents an ideal forecasting situation to challenge young minds.

When baby Anatol won't stop crying, his beleaguered mother seeks advice from an old woman known for her wisdom. She follows the old woman's counsel exactly, and soon, sure enough, little Anatol is quiet. But then the rest of the town's babies start wailing.

Challenge children to list the many causes and effects of the crying epidemic and perhaps suggest a solution before reading the ending. (Forecasting)

Sharmat, Marjorie Weinman. The 329th Friend. Illus. by
    Cyndy Szekeres. Four Winds, 1979.
    Emery Raccoon is convinced he is one of the most
boring of all creatures. He can't face another day with himself alone so he decides to have a party. His guest list grows
to include 328 assorted friends, from beetles to elephants.
    He prepares for the party by cooking mounds of food
(329 potatoes, 329 eggs, 329 tarts) and setting tables and ar-
ranging flowers. When he finds he doesn't have enough nap-
kins he tears up his bedsheets to provide for his friends.
Emery is filled with excitement as he waits for his guests to
arrive.
    The arrival sounds more like a marching army. Em-
ery graciously greets each one but he notices that the friendly
noise becomes more like a great roar as his 328 friends sit
down to eat. The crowd of animals is so noisy that Emery
can't get their attention even with his loudest voice. In des-
peration he decides to leave the party since his friends are
ignoring him. He dines alone in his house, listening to his
favorite music and conversing with himself. He is surprised
to find he is a rather entertaining fellow.
    Remembering his manners, he returns to his guests
in time to accept "thank you for a nice party" 328 times.
Emery decides the party was worth all the work as he has
discovered a friend he hadn't recognized before--himself--and
very good company he was after all. He now has 329 friends.
    Here is a delightful introduction to planning for very
young children. Giving a party for 328 friends requires considerable planning. Challenge children to discover what went
wrong with Emery's plans!

Singer, Isaac Bashevis. Why Noah Chose the Dove. Illus.
    by Eric Carle. Farrar, Straus and Giroux, 1973.
    An age-old story from the Bible is retold as a study
in personalities. Human traits of competition, envy, vanity
and conceit are portrayed in the form of the animals Noah
chose to save from the flood.
    The animals boasted of their own importance and be-
littled the others to justify their presence on the Ark. Size,
color and strength made no difference, as each creature displayed a pompous opinion of itself and no respect for the fine
qualities of the others. Elephants and mice, snakes and
earthworms compete for a place on the Ark in a vain and dis-
respectful manner.
    Only the dove remains silent on her perch on a branch.
She remarks to Noah that each creature has something to give

and there is no need to boast or compete with one another. Noah favors the dove for her modest and considerate attitude and selects her to be his messenger, and she remains to this day a symbol of peace.

The physical differences and the dialogue of the animals touch basic concepts of reasoning, understanding, and decision-making.

Stalder, Valerie. Even the Devil Is Afraid of a Shrew. Adapted by Ray Broekel. Illus. by Richard Brown. Addison-Wesley, 1970.

In this folktale of Lapland, Pava Jalvi is a peaceful, quiet man who loves to listen to the sweet voices of birds. Unfortunately, he is married to a very unpleasant woman, a real shrew. All she does is grumble and complain.

One morning as they journey from their home to pick some cloudberries, Pava Jalvi can stand it no longer and decides to take matters into his own hands. He pushes his wife into a deep hole and covers it with a stone.

Human nature being what it is, however, in time he misses his wife's nagging and decides to uncover the hole. The title of this hilarious tale should help students to predict what will emerge. Getting rid of his wife was one thing, but how does one get rid of the devil? Can young problem solvers devise a solution for Pava? (Problem solving)

Tompert, Ann. Charlotte and Charles. Illus. by the author. Crown, 1970.

Charlotte and Charles are two giants who live on an island. One day, to her great delight, Charlotte spots ships sailing into the island's harbor. Charles does not share her enthusiasm, noting that in the past, people they dealt with always turned against them. Charlotte is determined to make the new visitors welcome but Charles maintains his pessimistic view of human nature. At this point in the story, ask the children to decide what the two giants should do. Should they welcome the visitors? What might be the consequences? Should they hide and hope the visitors will leave? What will be the consequences of this? Did the children make the same decision the giants did? They will want to hear the rest of the story to find out! (Decision making)

Travers, P. L. Two Pairs of Shoes. Illus. by Leo and Diane Dillon. Viking Press, 1980.

From <u>Two Pairs of Shoes</u> by P. L. Travers, illustrated by Leo and Diane Dillon.

"Listen to the story of Abu Kassem, the merchant, known for his riches but also for his ragged slippers, the visible sign of his miserliness...."

"Listen to the story of Ayaz, once a poor shepherd, who also owns tattered shoes and who is now keeper of the King's treasures."

Two men and their shoes and why each treasures his worn and tattered possessions make profound stories. As the author reveals the difference in their views, deepest truths are also revealed, about the men and about life.

These are two perfect stories to savor, to compare and to think deeply about! Both provide opportunity for the reader to forecast the possible fate of the merchant and the shepherd. Only the very astute will be able to do so!

(Forecasting)

Van Aarle, Thomas F. Don't Put Your Cart Before the Horse Race. Illus. by Bob Barner. Houghton Mifflin, 1980.
This deceptively simple picture book calls into play numerous critical thinking skills. A horse race seems simple enough on the surface, but lack of planning and of developing rules causes problems to arise which need solutions. Decisions are made, some right, some wrong, and the reader is challenged to reverse thought again and again. Questions which remain unanswered include: Where should the race begin and where should it end? In which direction should the horses run? And which comes first, the horse or the cart? Obviously, in planning any kind of contest, rules are needed. Here, children will see the chaos that results when planning is overlooked! (Planning)

Van Allsburg, Chris. The Garden of Abdul Gasazi. Houghton Mifflin, 1979.
Sometimes the very thin line between illusion and reality is not as clearly defined as we would like it to be. It certainly isn't the day that Alan Mitz stumbles into the garden of Abdul Gasazi. For in this bizarre and eerie place, where strange topiary trees loom, the evil visage of Gasazi casts its shadows. In this tale of a small boy determined to rescue a neighbor's dog, Alan is faced with the problem of ignoring the sign on Gasazi's gate which reads, "Absolutely, Positively No Dogs Allowed In This Garden." He does enter the garden, but even after he has escaped the spell of Gasazi still seems to penetrate his everyday world.

Solving Alan's problem of rescuing the dog is com-

plicated, as the reader realizes that he has entered both the real and surreal world. The beautiful images created by the author/artist will continue to haunt the reader long after the enchanted garden has been left behind, leaving him or her to ponder whether or not Alan's problem was really resolved!
(Problem solving)

Van Woerkom, Dorothy. Alexandra the Rock-eater. Illus. by Rosekrans Hoffman. Knopf, 1978.

In tales where wishes come true, wishes can also get out of hand. When Alexandra and Igor fervently wish for one child to call their own, they are rewarded not with one, but one hundred! There is love enough for all of them, just room enough in the small house, but not food enough for so many hungry children and not a penny to buy more.

So, armed with only two small cheeses and a pocket-knife, Alexandra heads toward the dark side of the forest, determined to outwit a destructive dragon and capture his gold. In a funny and unusual twist, the dragon turns out to be young and dim-witted, and he decides to take Alexandra home to meet his Momma--a formidable foe indeed! How Alexandra outwits two dragons and acquires the gold makes a perfect problem to be solved. How fluently can children think to tackle this one? (Problem solving)

Waterton, Betty. A Salmon for Simon. Illus. by Ann Blades. Atheneum, 1980.

Problem-solving and decision-making skills are closely related and A Salmon for Simon deals with both. Simon is a small Canadian boy who fishes among the rocks on the beach near his home. One day an eagle drops a salmon into a small tidal pool. The water is scant and the beautiful fish is sure to die, for the tide is out and will not return in time to fill the pool. Simon might decide to tell his mother of his find and thus have fresh salmon for dinner. He could decide to leave the salmon to its fate. However, children looking at the beautiful illustrations will see the possibility of digging a trench to the sea to allow the salmon to escape. This is, of course, the decision that Simon makes. The children will share his joy when, after blisters and hours of work, the little Indian boy watches the salmon swim to the sea. Few children will disagree with the choice Simon made. A delightful story-hour book! (Decision making, Problem solving)

Wilde, Oscar. The Star Child. Illus. by Fiona French.
Four Winds Press, 1979.
Two woodcutters were making their way home one
snowy winter evening when a bright and beautiful star fell out
of the sky and into the pine forest before them. They ran
toward it, and found not a star, but a sleeping baby wrapped
in a cloak of golden tissue. One of the men took the baby
home.
The child was brought up with the village children, and
every year he grew more beautiful. But he also became vain
and selfish. And, as the child of a star, he was filled with
overweening pride.
One day, he accidentally meets his real mother, but
when she calls him her son he spurns her because she is old
and ugly and clothed in rags. For this cruel act, he is trans-
formed into a creature ugly as a toad.
As in most fine fairy tales, it is not the magic wand or
enchantment that allows the hero or heroine to emerge successfully, but the soul of man with all of the failings and greatness of human beings. In The Star Child, the reader is gently led through an examination of cause and effect, to the
realization of the value of humility and compassion. Jewell-
like paintings unfold the journey of the Star Child as he makes
his way through his medieval world.
This is a tale of many causes and effects (Cause: the
woodcutters found a child. Effect: they took the child home.
Cause: the child became vain and selfish. Effect: _____
_____.) How many cause and effect relationships can
children discover? (Forecasting)

Williams, Jay. Everyone Knows What a Dragon Looks Like.
Illus. by Mercer Mayer. Four Winds Press, 1976.
The author and illustrator combine their talents to
create an appealing story in an intriguing setting. Together
they blend fantasy with the realism of human nature to provide
an entertaining, colorful story.
In ancient China there lives a homeless but cheerful
boy. His job is to sweep the road that runs through the gate
to the city. One day a messenger arrives to warn the city
of an attack by the Wild Horsemen.
The incompetent men of the city can think of nothing
to save the city and pray to the Cloud Dragon for help. A
small, fat man appears, announcing that he is the answer to
their prayers. No one believes him and he is rudely asked
to leave. Only the boy offers him food and drink and kindness. At this point in the story children should have many

predictions as to the outcome. How can this small man save the city? What will the boy's role be? There are as many possibilities as there are young readers! (Forecasting)

Williams, Jay. The Reward Worth Having. Illus. by Mercer Mayer. Four Winds Press, 1977.
What kind of reward is truly worth having? As three soldiers of the King discover, it depends on what you value most in life!

The soldiers are marching home through a dark wood and hear faint cries of help. They come upon a tiny little man, "no bigger than a rabbit," whose long gray beard is stuck in the heavy stone door leading to his house. The soldiers soon set him free, and the grateful little man offers to let each soldier choose his own reward.

He escorts his three rescuers into a splendid gold and silver chamber, furnished with chairs and tables carved out of whole diamonds. The little man points to three bird cages. In one cage is a bird made of shining gold. In another, a bird made of iron, each feather and claw strongly etched. In the third is a small, gray bird, very much alive.

"Now," says the little man, "each of you may choose what you want most!"

Which would children choose and why? If each of the birds were evaluated by listing the same number of advantages and disadvantages of ownership, which would emerge the victor? In this tale of fantasy and suspense the author's resolution of choices may or may not be that of the reader. This is a book which will leave children with much to think about.
(Decision making, Evaluation)

Winthrop, Elizabeth. Journey to the Bright Kingdom. Illus. by Charles Mikola Ycak. Holiday House, 1979.
"Kiyo was born in May. When the little girl was laid beside her, the mother reached out and gently touched the baby's face with her fingertips, running her hands over the fine smooth skin and the small bump of a nose."

Kiyo's mother was blind, and her greatest sorrow was that she could not see her daughter. As Kiyo grew older, her mother would ask her to describe everything in the world around them. Then she would tell Kiyo of Kakure-sato, an underground kingdom ruled by mice where there is no sadness or sickness or blindness.

Kiyo discovers the kingdom for herself, and longs to make the journey there with her dying mother. Such an under-

taking, however, is forbidden by her father, who refuses to
believe in magical worlds. Young readers must decide with
Kiyo whether to risk the journey or not. (Decision making)

Wolkstein, Diane. The Red Lion. A Tale of Ancient Persia.
　　Illus. by Ed Young. Crowell, 1977.
　　　　Based on an old Persian story, probably a Sufi "teach-
ing-tale," The Red Lion tells of a long-ago prince who ran
away on the eve of his coronation. The reason for his flight
was simple. Prince Azgid was afraid. He could not face
the task set for him before he could become king. He could
not prove a bravery he did not have by fighting the ferocious
Red Lion. Yet, on his travels he finds many lions waiting
for him and learns that a lion will always be waiting until he
faces the first. Young minds are challenged to go far beyond
the literal meaning of this symbolic tale, and will find delight
in Ed Young's miniature style of art reflecting the ancient
Persian and Islamic manuscript paintings.
　　　　The tale presents a problem-solving exercise far more
difficult to deal with than problems which have extrinsic factors. The reader realizes early in the story that the problem
is not the lion to be faced, but a deep-rooted sense of fear
which must be overcome. How do we overcome our innermost
fears? A brainstorming session will reveal many approaches
to this basic problem. (Problem solving)

PART TWO

PROGRAMMING WITH BOOKS

CHAPTER 6

PUTTING IT ALL TOGETHER

The selection of picture books for use in programs for gifted children in the elementary and junior high school requires a different perspective on the part of the evaluator. The criteria and the annotated titles given thus far in this text should provide a starting point for the librarian or teacher challenged with this responsibility. Once selection has occurred, however, the development of the child's critical and productive thinking skills is not assured unless programming is designed to bring about the acquisition of these skills.

The literature units which follow deal with specific types of literature and with the works of selected authors to demonstrate how students may be helped to become critical readers and at the same time develop a love of reading and of books which will transform the reading process into a lifestyle rather than a skill.

The critical and productive thinking skills acquired in the reading and sharing of fine books can be applied to all areas of one's life; thus, the child who learns to plan, forecast, or solve problems in a literary situation can be helped to transfer these skills to life situations. In helping characters make judgments or decisions, the child is strengthening his or her own evaluative powers. It is interesting to note that several studies of adults who have made a significant impact on their fields of endeavor indicate that there is no correlation between school achievement and achievement in adult life. There is, however, a definite correlation between participation in extra-curricular activities and adult achievement. Good literature and the development of the child's personal reading as an extra-curricular activity may well have a significant impact on the future achievement of our gifted students. The units which follow are designed to help this goal become a reality.

THINKING SKILLS WITH FAIRY TALES

(From Thinking Skills with Fairy Tales, published by
BookLures, Inc. Used with permission)

Warm-Up Activities

1. Fluency: the ability to make many responses.
   a. List as many folk and fairy tales as you can.
   b. List all the folk and fairy tale objects you can think of that are magic.
   c. List as many folk and fairy tale characters as you can.

2. Flexibility: the ability to respond in a variety of areas.
   a. Categorize the fairy tales you listed in the fluency activity (1.a.) How many categories do you have?
   b. Look at your list of categories. Did you list tall tales? animal tales? tales of enchantment? What other categories can be added?
   c. Match a modern invention of today with a folk or fairy tale character who might need the invention to solve his or her problem. Match as many characters and inventions as you can.

3. Originality: responding in new or unique ways.
   a. "What fairy or folk tale (Fluency 1.a.) did you list that you think no one else listed?"
   b. "What magic object do you think is your most unusual?" (Fluency 1.b.)
   c. "Suppose the wicked queen in Snow White became so angry with her mirror that she smashed it to pieces. How else could she find out if she were the 'fairest in the land'?
   d. "What new idea could our class think of to rescue Rapunzel from her tower?"

4. Elaboration: adding to basic ideas.
   a. "Choose a magic object from your list. (Fluency 1.b.) How could you elaborate on that object?" (Story? Sentence? Picture? Poem? Song?)
   b. Hold up a folk tale with an unattractive cover. "How could we elaborate on this cover to make it more interesting and attractive?"
   c. "How many ways can we think of to show how truly

happy the Ugly Duckling must have been when it discovered it was a swan?"

5. Evaluation: examining positive and negative aspects.
(When introducing evaluation, to avoid prejudice, push
students to strive for the same number of positive and
negative points.)
   a. "Choose a magic object from your list (Fluency 1. b.).
   Use the evaluation 'T' to list the desirable things
   about the object and the undesirable things about it."

Flying Carpet

Example: _____

Desirable   Undesirable

   b. "Suppose you had a magic mirror which would show
   you what was happening anywhere in the world. What
   would be desirable about it? What would be undesirable about it?"
   c. Evaluate a book or a character from a fairy tale the
   class has read. "What did you find that was good
   about the story (or character)? What was bad about
   the book?"

Communication

1. Description within given categories:
"One part of communication is using descriptive words.
Think of the wicked queen in Snow White. What words
might describe how she looks? What words describe
how she feels?"

2. Description of feelings:
"Describe how Cinderella felt when her stepsisters went
to the ball and she was left at home. Try to think of
words to accurately describe her feelings."

3. Comparisons/Relationships:
"What words can you think of to finish this sentence:
The fairy godmother's wand sparkled like ...."

4. Empathy:

Empathy does not lend itself to written activity. It is most effectively developed when it is positively reinforced as it occurs in the classroom.

5. Composition:
"As I came around the corner of the school this morning, there on the playground was the strangest creature I had ever seen."

6. Non-verbal:
"Show me, using your face, how you would feel if you were the Ugly Duckling. Add your hands and body to help show. Now pretend you have become a swan. Show how you feel."

Planning: identifying steps, materials, and problems necessary for task completion.

"If I were to make a magic brew, what materials would I need? What steps would I follow? What different kinds of problems might I have?" (Allow for response after each step.) "What would this brew be used for?"

"We need to spin straw into gold. Let's plan how we will proceed. What materials will we need? What steps should we take? What problems might we have?" (Allow for response after each step.)

Forecasting: ability to link cause and effect.

"A king has lost his crown. What caused him to lose it? What effects might this have? Choose the most interesting cause and effect. Defend your choice with at least three reasons."

"It rained feathers last night. What are all the reasons for this? (causes). What are all the things that will happen because it rained feathers? (effects). Choose the best cause and effect. Defend your choices with at least three reasons."

Decision making: ability to establish criteria for making choices.

"We have read many interesting folk and fairy tales.
Which one do you think is the best? Think of three
stories that you like. (These are your alternatives.)
Consider the following criteria as you make your choice:
1. Does it have a good ending?
2. Did it keep me interested?
3. Would I recommend it to a friend?
Give three reasons for your choice. "

Problem solving: the ability to identify a problem, examine
many alternatives for a solution, and arrive at a solution
which meets established criteria.
Define the basic problem presented in many nursery
rhymes. Brainstorm for solutions.
1. Humpty Dumpty. How could he be put back together again?
2. Little Miss Muffet. What is her basic problem?
How can she solve it?
3. Mary, Mary, Quite Contrary. What is the problem? Whose problem is it? How many solutions
can we find?

I. YOU'RE INVITED

Divide the class into four groups. Each group receives
a "Would you rather?" card. The groups are to rank the
items on the card in order of group preference. Three reasons should be given for the selection of the first choice
item.

A. WOULD YOU RATHER EAT
_____ fried worms _____ mud pies
_____ Tarantula stew _____ alligator steak

B. WOULD YOU RATHER LIVE
_____ in an underground mole kingdom
_____ in an ice queen's palace
_____ in a mermaid's cave
_____ on a pirate ship

C. WOULD YOU RATHER BE
_____ asleep for 100 years
_____ the owner of a magic touch that turns everything
to gold

_____ able to turn princes into frogs
_____ the possessor of eternal youth

D.   WOULD YOU RATHER HELP
_____ a witch prepare a magic brew
_____ Robin Hood steal from the rich to give to the
poor
_____ Santa's elves make holiday candy
_____ Sir Gawain slay the monster dragon

II.   HOORAY!

You have just won one of the following prizes. For fifteen minutes meet with a group of classmates. Decide on the first two prizes your group would choose. Decision must be unanimous! Give reasons for your choices.

A.   _____ A sword which slays any enemy it touches
B.   _____ A potion to give one the strength of ten men
C.   _____ A pitcher of fresh, sweet milk which never empties
D.   _____ A ring which grants three wishes
E.   _____ Magic boots which transport the wearer to any place he or she desires in seconds
F.   _____ A cloak of invisibility
G.   _____ A book containing all the wisdom of the ages
H.   _____ A treasure map with directions to a chest of gold

III.   THE THINKER'S MOTHER GOOSE

Many Mother Goose rhymes present problems with no solutions. Brainstorm with a friend or the class to come up with possible solutions to these problems:

MARY MARY QUITE CONTRARY
HOW DOES YOUR GARDEN GROW
WITH SILVER BELLS AND COCKLE SHELLS
AND PRETTY MAIDS ALL IN A ROW

What will Mary do with rows of pretty young women: How will she feed and shelter them? Will she soon run out of land with rows and rows of pretty maids?

> LITTLE MISS MUFFET
> SAT ON A TUFFET
> EATING HER CURDS AND WHEY
> WHEN ALONG CAME A SPIDER
> AND SAT DOWN BESIDE HER......

What will Miss Muffet do now? How can she prevent this from happening again?

> RUB A DUB DUB, THREE MEN IN A TUB
> AND WHO DO YOU THINK THEY BE?
> THE BUTCHER, THE BAKER, THE CANDLESTICK
>   MAKER
> TURN 'EM OUT, KNAVES ALL THREE!

What will the men need to take with them to survive on the open sea for several days? Design a new tub which will better provide for their needs.

> PETER PETER PUMPKIN EATER
> HAD A WIFE AND COULDN'T KEEP HER
> PUT HER IN A PUMPKIN SHELL
> AND THERE HE KEPT HER VERY WELL

How does Peter's wife feel about this imprisonment? Plan a sure-fire escape for her. What will she need? Who, if anyone, will help her?

IV.   THE REAL MOTHER GOOSE

Throughout the ages people have often found humor in serious situations. Such humor can take the form of jokes, riddles or rhymes. Many of the Mother Goose rhymes were written to poke fun at the leaders or the problems of a particular time in history.

Below you will discover the real meaning of several familiar rhymes. You will find it interesting to search in your school or public library for the history of other rhymes.

Study each rhyme and its meaning, the modern parody given, and try writing your own parody of a familiar rhyme. Include in your parody a major concern of the people of our time.

A. In the days of King Henry VIII a servant, John Horner, was sent to London with a pie for the King. Important papers giving land ownership were baked in the pie. When the pie arrived, no papers were found. To this day the Horner family owns the Estate in question.

Little Jack Horner	He stuck in his thumb
Sat in the corner	He pulled out a plum
Eating his Christmas Pie.	And said, "What a good boy am I!"

B. Queen Elizabeth of England was said to tease her ministers as a cat plays with a mouse. She also loved to dance to fiddle music. Her royal ladies always tasted her food first. The soup taster was called the spoon and the man who brought the food was called the dish. One day the two ran away to marry.

Hey diddle, diddle	The little dog laughed
The cat and the fiddle	to see such sport
The cow jumped over	And the dish ran away
the moon	with the spoon

C. Try a parody

Rain rain go away
Come again another day
Don't remind me of the fate
Of those involved in Watergate

Exhaust when it's hot
Smoke when it's cold
Pollution simmers in the pot
Five decades old
No one likes it hot
No one likes it cold
But people keep polluting
So the Story's told

V. THE LITTLE MERMAID - HANS CHRISTIAN ANDERSEN

The following lines are from Andersen, the master teller of original tales. He truly paints a picture with words.

Here is the description of the scene as the Little Mermaid approaches the undersea abode of the horrible seawitch.

Choose colorful words to describe this scene. Read The Little Mermaid and compare your choice with the author's.

The Little Mermaid went out of her _____ and swam toward the _____ whirlpool where the sea witch lived. No _____ grew there, only ____ _____, _____ sand stretched toward the pool, where the water like a _____ whirled around. She travelled a path of _____ slime. The trees on either side reached out like _____ with _____ arms. Everyone of them had caught something. There were _____ and _____ clutched tight and skeletons of _____ she came to a large clearing in the _____ where _____ watersnakes wallowed in the mud showing their _____ bellies. In the middle of the clearing stood a house made of _____ and there sat the _____ seawitch with a _____ in her mouth, a _____ round her neck and _____ which covered her hands and feet.

VI.   347 CINDERELLAS

There are over 347 versions of the Cinderella tale found throughout the world. Here are basic elements of eight of these tales. How many can you match?

A.   Country

a.   American Indian   e.   Ireland
b.   Czechoslovakia   f.   Russia
c.   China   g.   Vietnam
d.   Egypt   h.   Germany

B.   Name

a.   Tattercoats   f.   Rhodopis
b.   Turkey Girl   g.   Marushka
c.   Tam   h.   Ashputtel
d.   Vasilisa   i.   Other
e.   Shih Chieh

C. **Scorned By**

a. Stepmother
b. Stepsisters
c. Half sister
d. Grandfather
e. Other

D. **Tasks**

a. Herd turkeys
b. Tend rice plants
c. Scrub the hearth
d. Secure a light from a witch
e. Weave fine linen
f. Find apples, violets, strawberries under the snow
g. Pick peas out of ashes
h. Other

E. **Wishes**

a. To be the number one daughter
b. To go to a ball
c. To meet the king
d. To attend a feast
e. To complete an impossible task
f. To be freed from slavery

F. **Helped By**

a. Messenger from Heaven
b. Magical fish
c. Enchanted bird
d. Cloud fairy
e. Fairy godmother
f. Glowing skull
g. Gobbler
h. Gooseherd
i. Magical pipe
j. Hazel tree

G. Use elements from each list and combine them in original and different ways or add your own twists to the story.

BE SURE TO ......

1. Give your heroine (or hero) an original and fitting name.
2. Create a unique setting for the story.
3. Who rejects your main character and why?
4. What tasks must he or she perform? What will happen if these tasks are not done on time or not done well?
5. What does the hero or heroine long for?

6. Who helps him or her achieve the wish?
7. How is the hero or heroine helped?
8. What happens at the end of the story? To the hero or heroine? To those who scorned him or her?

Think in original ways! For example, does the trouble-maker in the story have to be a person?

VII. EPITAPH

Rubbings from gravestones often reveal interesting facts about a person or the time in which he or she lived.

Write epitaphs for three fairy or folktale characters.

Be sure your lines or verse reveal something about the character or his or her life.

Epitaphs are usually very short.

Every word is important.

VIII. INCANTATIONS

"Some devils ask but the parings of one's nail.
A rush, a hair, a drop of blood, a pin
A nut, a cherry stone."--William Shakespeare

Folk and fairy tales abound with magic brews and incantations to bring forth their magic properties.

A. Plan a magic brew
B. List ingredients to use
C. What problems would arise in obtaining these ingredients?
D. What effect would the brew have on the user?

Ingredients	Problems in Obtaining

E.   Compose an incantation to make the brew effective

IX.   THE OTHER SIDE OF THE STORY

Writers of folktales often present characters as either good or bad. "Good" characters can do no wrong. For example, it is perfectly acceptable for the hero to trick the witch or dragon but wrong for the witch or dragon to resort to trickery.

Here is a possible "other side of the story" as told by the queen in Snow White.

Read the story below and select your favorite fairy tale villain to transform into a hero or heroine by telling his or her side of the story.

THE MISUNDERSTOOD QUEEN

When I married the king and became Snow White's step-mother I truly loved the beautiful little girl as my own child. It was by accident one night that I overheard her talking to the ravens who, for some strange reason, gathered often at her window.

Imagine my shock to discover this lovely child chanting evil spells. First she wished upon her father both illness and death, and upon me, ugliness of such immense proportion that the entire kingdom would shun me.

To my dismay and sorrow, my beloved husband sickened and died before the year was out. Thus, I often consulted by mirror to see the first traces of the spell she had cast on me. One day I saw it! A small mole appeared just below my right eye and I knew indeed that Snow White was an evil witch whose purpose was to destroy the kingdom. I had no choice but to order her killed by the huntsman.

X.   THE STAR CHILD

Forecasting

Oscar Wilde has written a haunting tale about a baby wrapped in a golden cloak who is found on a cold, winter

night in the middle of the forest by two woodsmen. The child
is raised by the villagers but as his beauty increases, so does
his pride and selfishness. One day an ugly beggar-woman arrives in the village claiming the child as her son. What will
this child, who "scorns the small and helpless creatures of
the earth, and takes delight in acts of cruelty," do? What
will happen as a result of his action?

CAUSE	EFFECT
Child found in forest	Taken to village and cared for
Child's beauty grows	Becomes vain and selfish
Shows off and performs cruel acts	Other children follow his example

XI. ACRONYMS

Acronyms have become a way of life in our society.
Daily references in the news to HUD or HEW or IRS are common. What acronyms would fit the well-known folk and fairy
tale characters given here?

Example:

Fairy tale witches might belong to S. P. E. L. L.,
an organization devoted to:
Scientifically
Perfect
Enchantments
Lacking
Love

Decide what each of the letters stand for in the acronyms given below.

A.   The seven dwarfs belong to the miner's union,
      M. I. N. E.

_____

B.   Casey belongs to the baseball team, O. U. T.

_____

C.   Railroad men, John Henry and Casey Jones, belong
      to P. U. S. H.

_____

D.   Robin Hood and his merry band belong to L. O. O. T.

_____

E.   The Wizard of Oz belongs to the Wizard's Union,
      F. A. K. E.

_____

F.   Paul Bunyan and other lumber men belong to L. O. G.

_____

XII.   PROBLEM SOLVING

   Step One: State the facts leading to the problem.   Who?
      What? When? Where? Why?

   Step Two: What is the actual problem.   Can you state
      the problem in two or three different ways? Is there
      more than one problem to solve to achieve the major
      solution?

   Step Three: List as many solutions as you can to the
      problem.   Do not reject a single idea.

   Step Four: Examine each solution listed in light of what
      you want the solution to accomplish.   Select those
      which meet the criteria you have established for the
      solution.

   Step Five: Select the one solution which seems best.

Step Six: List all the steps you must take to implement
the solution. Include any objects, people or material
you will need to carry out your plan.

XIII. PICK A PROBLEM!

In the hero tale the hero or heroine confronts many
problems. While some of these problems have to do with
magic or enchantment, the hero or heroine usually is without
magic powers. Choose a problem card and using the guide
to problem solving, work out a solution to the problem. Work
alone or with a friend or friends.

A. The hero or heroine must discover why the shoes of
twelve princesses are worn out nightly when they are
locked securely in their room each evening.

B. The Hand. The hero or heroine arrives at a house
with no children, for every new-born child is spirited
away by a giant hand which comes down the chimney.

C. The hero or heroine keeps watch in a chapel near the
coffin of a beautiful princess, who nightly rises to
slay any who are brave enough to guard her.

D. A hero or heroine enters a land in mourning because
its prince has been spirited away by ugly trolls, who
keep him in an enchanted sleep in a dark cave. The
king offers half his hingdom to any who can find and
rescue the missing prince.

E. A dreadful and dangerous monster dwells in the dungeon of the king's palace. The king refuses permission for the princess to marry her childhood sweetheart unless the monster is first overcome.

XIV. THE TOWER

When Rapunzel was twelve years old an enchantress
shut her into a tower thirty feet in height and with sides as
slick as glass all around. It had neither stairs nor door,
but at the top was a little window.

SUPPOSE.... The tower were located on an island completely surrounded by water and located one hundred

miles from any other land source.

SUPPOSE.... The water surrounding the island were infested with man-eating sharks.

SUPPOSE.... No ship owner would agree to take you in his ship for fear of reprisals from the enchantress.

HOW WOULD YOU RESCUE RAPUNZEL?

A. What are the basic problems to overcome?
   1.
   2.
   3.
   4.

B. What can you do to solve each problem?
   1.
   2.
   3.
   4.

C. Make a list of all materials or equipment you would need to accomplish the rescue. Note the use of each.

XV. MYTHOLOGICAL TIC TAC TOE

Complete any three squares down, across or diagonally. Consult the section on MYTHS (Dewey 200s) in your school or public library.

ALL ABOUT _____
(God or Goddess)

Describe both the powers and weaknesses of this God or Goddess.	How would friends describe this character?	Find another story about this character. What new facts did you find about him or her?
How would enemies describe this character?	At what point in his-her life did this person receive unusual powers? How were they received?	Would this character's powers be useful in today's society? How?
Design a family tree for this character.	What major problem(s) did this character have to solve?	Summarize the basic story plot by writing it as a current motion picture ad. Who might play the major parts?

XVI. ROLE PLAY

Role play gives students an opportunity to involve themselves totally in a situation ... to think, feel and act as others
would in the same situation. Effective role-play incorporates
the critical thinking skills of fluency, flexibility, originality,
elaboration and instant decision-making and/or problem-
solving. It is an ideal teaching method to get students to
"think on their feet" and to use the thinking skills which have
been practiced.

The following activity, The Drum Beater of Suckatash,
provides an ideal role-play situation involving the entire class.
The story should be read aloud and the basic problems of the
story identified. Be sure the students identify the theme of
the story--which is the need to honor written or verbal con-
tracts.

The story can also serve as a model for developing a
parody of an old tale. Students should be able to recognize
the parody here of "The Pied Piper of Hamelin." Ask them
to identify those elements of the story which have been re-
tained and those which have been changed. Caution students
that in writing a parody, enough of the original must remain
so that the parody can be recognized.

A MODERN PARODY

The Drum Beater of Suckatash

The happy and productive people of the town of Suckatash made their entire living by producing the biggest and
most delicious squash in all the land. Indeed, kings sent
their couriers from great distances to obtain it, princesses
cried for it, and no wizard or witch was ever able to duplicate its succulent quality.

Now it happened one fateful summer day that a blight
of flies descended upon the town and began to destroy the
prize crop. The people hovered about in a frenzy, attacking
the flies with flyswatters and insect spray, but to no avail.
With heavy hearts and tears streaming down their faces, the
townspeople appealed to the Mayor and Aldermen to find a
solution to the horrible problem. But alas, no solution was
forthcoming and just as the crop seemed surely to be doomed,
salvation entered the town meeting in the form of Pierre Bombassa, composer of The Fly Sonata in E Minor. Although he

was the town outcast, Pierre truly loved the squash crop and for a fee of 100 francs per year plus all the squash he could eat, Pierre offered to rid the town of the plague.

The Aldermen, having little faith in Pierre, but having nothing to lose but the crop (which would be lost anyway), agreed to Pierre's terms. Pierre set to work. He spent all night banging a huge drum and howling his recently composed sonata. By morning the flies were gone. The townfolk could not decide if it was the drum, the song, or the terrible voice of Pierre that drove off the flies. But the buzzing insects were gone--that much was positive.

When Pierre again appeared before the Aldermen to collect his fee, none could recollect promising any fee at all. They laughed at the ragged man, leaving him standing, with empty pockets, in the middle of the Town Hall as they went out to join the celebration.

That night Pierre set to work. He cut down all the squash plants and set fire to the remaining stalks. In the morning the squash fields lay black and barren and Pierre was gone. He left a note saying only: "VIVE LA SQUASH!"

ROLE PLAY

The Town Meeting of Suckatash

The citizens of the town of Suckatash are violently angry at the loss of their prize crop and their anger is directed not so much at Pierre Bombassa as at the Town Aldermen who refused to pay him the amount they had promised. Four class members are chosen to play the parts of the Aldermen and to defend themselves against the town's wrath. Class members play the parts of the townspeople and can ask any questions they wish. The class may vote at the end of the town meeting on the Alderman who best defended himself. The cards which follow reveal the ulterior motives of the Aldermen for the action they took. These cards should be given only to those playing the parts.

THE STORE OWNER

You run the only store in Suckatash and are the brother-in-law of the plant manager. You make a good profit selling fly swatters and insect spray. Although you always smile when serving your customers, the size of your smile is only exceeded by the size of your prices. You are regarded as a very jolly fellow in the town.

THE PLANT MANAGER

You get re-elected as Alderman each year by giving out prize squash during election year. You have purchased stock in a fly swatter factory and have arranged exclusive sales to your brother-in-law, the storekeeper. You are a very tight-lipped person but are considered level-headed. You often hesitate before you speak but people usually listen to what you have to say. You often throw a "wet blanket" on others' ideas.

MUNICIPAL LAWYER

You are a smooth operator with great political ambitions. You need the support of the people in order to get elected to the post of county supervisor. You did not want to pay Pierre to rid the town of the flies because you were working on a plan which would make you the hero of the day. Pierre's grand solution robbed you of the glory you expected. You are very adept at placing blame on others and twisting what others say to make them appear in an unfavorable light.

LEADER OF THE SQUASH HARVESTING AND WINE-MAKING UNION (SQUASH STOMPERS LOCAL #448)

Just before Pierre appeared on the scene you had perfected a plan which would require additional dues from union members to be used to hire a squash expert from Spain to rid the town of flies. Actually you had planned to adopt a clever disguise, attempt in vain to drive away the flies, then disappear. You would thus be considerably richer for trying. You tend to blame any and all disasters on "big business" and/or the lack of effective government programs to help the working man.

XVII. SOME MODERN VERSIONS OF OLD TALES--TOO GOOD TO MISS

Ardizzone's Hans Christian Andersen: Fourteen Classic Tales. Atheneum, 1979.
    A retelling in rich language and lovely mood drawings. Superb, beautiful and haunting.

Andersen's The Snow Queen. Retold by Naomi Lewis. Illus. by Errol Le Cain. Viking, 1979.

A natural for problem-solving activities as little Gerda overcomes many obstacles in rescuing Kay. Magnificent illustrations!

The Riddle of the Drum, by Verna Aardema. Illus. by Tony Chen. Four Winds Press, 1979.
The colorful Mexican version of "The Fool of the World and the Flying Ship". Well-told and useful for analysis of likenesses and differences of the two tales.

Why the Tides Ebb and Flow, by Joan Bowden. Illus. by Marc Brown. Houghton Mifflin, 1979.
An old woman's search for a hut causes the tides to ebb and flow. An excellent model for original stories which explain occurrences in nature.

In the Land of the Small Dragon, by Ann Clark. Viking, 1979.

Tattercoats, by Flora Steel, Bradbury, 1976.

Vasilisa the Beautiful, by Thomas Whitney, Macmillan, 1970.
The Vietnamese, Welsh and Russian versions of Cinderella. Excellent for comparison with Perrault's tale.

Exceptional retellings of Grimm's tales: Great for problem solving!

The Twelve Dancing Princesses. Illus. by Errol Le Cain. Viking, 1978.
The Seven Ravens, by Donna Diamond. Viking, 1979.
Hansel and Gretel. Illus. by Lisbeth Zwerger. Morrow, 1979.
The Bearskinner, by Felix Hoffman. Atheneum, 1978.
The Sleeping Beauty. Illus. by Warwick Hutton. Atheneum, 1979.
Snow White. Trans. by Paul Heins. Illus. by Trina Hyman. Little, 1974.

And five more!

Errol Le Cain. The Cabbage Princess. Faber and Faber, 1969.
A study in design, and in 17th-century costume and customs.

Mercer Mayer. Beauty and the Beast. Four Winds, 1978.

Ann McGovern. Half A Kingdom. Warne, 1977.
    The female heroine!

Oscar Wilde. The Star Child. Illus. by Fiona French.
    Four Winds, 1979.

Carolyn Haywood. The King's Monster. Morrow, 1980.

THINKING SKILLS WITH FANTASY

I. THE TEA PARTY

You have as guests at a tea party the following characters:

1. A cuddly brown bear who talks
2. A cat named Sam
3. A 2-inch mouse named Stuart
4. An unstuffed scarecrow
5. A small person who always borrows things
6. A large white rabbit with a pocket watch

A. What do you think they could talk about?

B. What kinds of food from the four food groups would you serve?

C. What kinds of manners do you think the guests will have?

D. How would a cuddly brown bear introduce himself? How would this introduction be different from the way Sam would introduce himself? (Originality, Fluency)

E. How can you work out a workable seating plan for this party?

F. Draw a diagram of a seating plan for the guests at your party. Be sure to consider any problems which might arise if some guests are seated too close to each other.

II. FANTASY COLLAGE

A. List as many human characters from fantasy books as you can.

B. Now list as many characters (human or animal) as you can which begin with the letters in the word "fantasy".

F

A

N

T

A

S

Y

C. Choose three of the characters you named above and create a collage which you feel says something about this character. It does not have to necessarily be a picture of the character. (Fluency, Flexibility, Originality, Synthesis)

III. CREATE A STORY

Back in 1726 when Jonathan Swift wrote Gulliver's Travels, sea travel was the most exciting method of travel. In this story, the hero is a shipwrecked sailor who discovers strange lands and strange civilizations such as the tiny Lilliputians and the huge Brobdignagians.

A. YOU are a modern day author, writing in the tradition of Jonathan Swift.

B. Your main character (hero or heroine) is a Space Traveler of the future, whose space ship carries him (or her) beyond the limits of our solar system, out into the realm of the stars.

C. Imagine what strange forms of life or civilizations he (or she) may find on the revolving planets of some distant sun (which to us is a star in the night sky).

D. The form of your story should be as follows:

1. Your space traveler needs to keep a Journal, telling of all discoveries made. He (or she) visits several planets of the distant star.
2. Write a brief journal entry about what kind of life he (or she) finds on each planet visited.
3. Each planet's life forms will be different from all the others. (Originality, Elaboration)

IV. FANTASY ROCK

A. Pretend you are a television producer. You have just read a terrific book that you want to make a rock opera of. The book is:

_____
(choose a fantasy book)

by

_____

B. Decide who will sing each of the songs listed below. (This must be a character from your fantasy book.) Also decide what scene the song will best fit into.

Song Title	Sung by	Scene
Cruel to be kind		
Another one bites the dust		
If you leave me now		
I'd love you to want me		
Three times in love		
Jet airline		
Long time		

C. Pretend the author of the book that you chose is coming to see your rock opera. You learn the night of the opening performance that this author will be in the audience.

D. What things can you do to honor him or her. These things need to be more than a simple introduction. (Planning, Originality, Analysis)

V.   THE STRANGE VISITOR

Complete after reading <u>Mary Poppins</u>, by P. L. Travers.

Carl Sagan, the famous American astronomer, writes to your school and says that on a distant planet in a remote galaxy, a new form of life has been found.

This new form of life is an absolutely perfect female being who flies through space with an umbrella.

Furthermore, Dr. Sagan informs your school that she is coming to visit.

A.   What effect would this amazing visit have on your school day?
B.   What effect would this discovery have on the study of astronomy from now on?
C.   How will you communicate with this lady?
D.   What effect will this lady have on the community in which your school is located?
E.   How will you deal with people in the community who are showing prejudice towards this unusual lady?
F.   What could you give her as a souvenir of your school? Of your home? (Forecasting, Problem solving)

VI.   THE LITTLE PEOPLE

To be completed after reading <u>The Borrowers</u> by Mary Norton.

A.   List as many small things as you can think of that the Borrowers would probably like to borrow.

B.   If you were a Borrower, what places in a house would you find the most dangerous?

C.   In <u>The Borrowers</u> by Mary Norton, Pod and Homily have not told Arrietty, as the story begins, about the great dangers in their lives. When do you think a child should be told these things? Do you think that "borrowing" is to stealing as "fantasy" is to lying? Tell why.

D.   What would be the advantages and disadvantages of having Borrowers in your house?

E.   Design a map showing the routes which the Borrowers would take in <u>your</u> house. Draw on the map the ob-

jects that would be taken. Put an estimate on the map telling how long you think it would take a Borrower to reach each of the rooms in the house.
(Originality, Fluency, Elaboration)

VII. I LIKE THIS ANIMAL!

A. List all the animal characters in the fantasy stories you have read.

B. What categories of fantasy do your fantasy stories fit into?
Examples: humorous fantasy, talking beast stories, adventures, mysteries.

C. Which of the animal characters would you most like to know personally?

D. Create a short poem expressing why you chose that animal. The poem should be composed in the following format:

1st line	(noun)	1 word
2nd line	(adjectives)	2 words
3rd line	(verbs)	3 words
4th line	(showing emotion, feelings)	4 words
5th line	(noun which is synonym for line 1)	1 word

Here is an example:
friend
brown, cuddly
grumbling, playing, dangling
happy to be him
Pooh
(Fluency, Flexibility, Originality, Elaboration)

VIII. HOW DOES IT FEEL?

To be completed after reading Sam, Bangs & Moonshine by Evaline Ness.
An important part of communication is description of feelings. In Sam, Bangs & Moonshine, Sam's father must

leave the house one rainy, stormy night to go and look for Sam's friend, Thomas, and Bangs the cat.

A. One of the following paragraphs describes how Sam felt, as the author described it.
   1. "Sam felt bad when her father left the house."
                          or
   2. "When her father had gone, Sam sat down. She listened to the rain hammer on the tin roof. Then suddenly it stopped. Sam closed her eyes and mouth, tight. She waited in the quiet room. It seemed to her that she waited forever."

B. Which of the above passages best describes Sam's feelings? Why? (Only one is a quote from the book itself.)

C. What other words could you write to describe her feelings? Fill in the blanks below:

Sam felt _____ . She had never felt so _____ before. Her _____ was _____, and her _____ was also _____. The _____ was _____. She _____ and _____ for a long time.

Can you continue this story?
(Communication-Empathy, Description)

IX. LEAVE A MESSAGE GAME

A. Write the names of five human fantasy characters in left hand column of a pro-con T.

B. Write the names of five animal fantasy characters in the right column.

C. Write a message for each character in the left column to send to a character in the right column. In the messages you may not use the names of the characters, because your classmates will have to guess who the message is to and who it is from.

D. Each message must have something to do with the characters, so that it will give your classmates a clue.

E. Which of your messages would be the most pleasing to the recipient (person receiving message)?

F. Which message would you be happy to receive? Why? (Originality, Fluency, Elaboration, Evaluation)

X. JUST SUPPOSE....

Before breakfast one day, Fern, the little girl in Charlotte's Web by E. B. White, saved a tiny pig's life. Later Wilbur the pig, goes to live on a nearby farm and is befriended by a spider named Charlotte. Fern goes to visit Wilbur every day.

A. SUPPOSE.... Fern had not gotten up early in the morning on the day her father went out to the pigpen and discovered that the baby pigs had been born.

B. SUPPOSE.... There wasn't a farmer nearby to sell Wilbur to. What else could Fern have done?

C. SUPPOSE.... Charlotte had been a bad-tempered spider.

D. SUPPOSE.... The day Wilbur escaped, he hadn't been caught.

E. How would you keep Fern and Wilbur together?

F. Write your own version of the story, using the above supposes.

G. In the original story:
1. What was the main problem? Can you state it in two or three different ways?
2. What led to the problem?
3. List several solutions to the problem.
4. Tell which solution you think is best.
5. List all of the things that need to be done to carry out this solution. Be sure to include names of people or things needed to successfully carry out this solution.   (Forecasting)

XI. SILLY THINGS TO DO!

A. In Charlotte's Web by E. B. White, the pig, Wilbur, tries to spin a web! What might these other fantasy book characters try to do that would be equally silly?
   The Cowardly Lion in the Wizard of Oz by Frank Baum.
   Bangs, the cat, in Sam, Bangs & Moonshine by Evelyn Ness.
   Eeyore, the donkey, in Winnie the Pooh by A. A. Milne.
   Fern, the little girl, in Charlotte's Web.

B. These strange activities don't have to be part of the original story. You can change the story to suit your silly activity.

C. Explain why each character would want to do this activity.
   Example: Mr. Banks in Mary Poppins might take his large black umbrella up to the rooftop and try to fly. His reason for doing this silly thing might be because he is jealous of Mary Poppins who can do this.   (Originality, Analysis)

THINKING SKILLS WITH HUMOROUS BOOKS

Developing productive and critical thinking skills should be a challenging and fun experience. Especially useful in beginning experiences with these skills are books with a humorous flavor because these provide an appealing base for both students and teachers. Many, many titles are appropriate. The titles and activities given here are intended as examples and as a starting point for the development of activities centered around other favorites.

I. List as many funny characters as you can think of. They can be from movies, books, comics, or TV.

_____   _____

_____   _____

II.   Now that your list is made, circle all of your characters that are from books. Can you think of any other funny characters from books that you have read to add to your list?

_____   _____
_____   _____
_____   _____
_____   _____

B Is for Betsy

by Carolyn Haywood

Betsy has done some things that she should be rewarded for. Inscribe the prize cups below with appropriate categories that you think Betsy might have won for herself.

Beezus and Ramona

by Beverly Cleary

Beezus' biggest problem was her little sister Ramona. Beezus was very patient with Ramona, but eventually she decided she did not like Ramona at all. How could a four-year-old be such a pest? Beezus knows sisters are supposed to love each other all the time, but with a sister like Ramona, it seemed impossible.

Below is Ramona's name. Beside each letter of her name, write a word that begins with that letter to describe Ramona.

R
A
M
O
N
A

Ellen Tebbits

by Beverly Cleary

Ellen Tebbits had one wish, that she and Austine Allen

were friends. The two girls had been best friends. They shared all kinds of secrets and adventures. They even wore the same dress the first day of school. But that day they had a terrible quarrel. Ellen slapped Austine! Ellen knew it was her fault but she didn't know how to begin to say she was sorry.

List the many ways in which Ellen could apologize to Austine.

Ellen Tebbits and Ramona Quimby

Below are a list of things done by either Ramona or Ellen. Place a check (√) under the name of the person who would most likely do this.

	Ramona	Ellen
1. Locked Ribsy in the bathroom.	———	———
2. Took horse-riding lessons	———	———
3. "Secret underwear" caused 2 people to be friends.	———	———
4. Launched a campaign to stop her father from smoking.	———	———
5. Wanted to be the teacher's pet.	———	———
6. Baked her rubber doll into a birthday cake.	———	———
7. Invited fourteen nursery school friends to a party without telling anyone.	———	———
8. Took dancing lessons.	———	———

Eddie's Happenings

by Carolyn Haywood

Things are always happening around Eddie. Below, you are going to make a poem about Eddie Wilson. The poem is called a cinquain. Follow the directions beside each line so that you can write your poem.

_____ (1 word--noun)

_____ (2 words--adjectives describing Eddie)

_____   (3 words--verbs)

_____   (4 words--describing, showing feeling)

_____   (1 word--synonym of first line)

Homer Price

by Robert McCloskey

One day Homer Price decided to help his Uncle Ulysses in his lunch room. Uncle Ulysses is a man with advanced ideas and a weakness for labor-saving devices. His lunch room is equipped with an automatic dishwasher, an automatic coffee maker, automatic toasters, and an automatic doughnut maker. While cleaning the doughnut machine, Uncle Ulysses asked Homer to finish putting in the last few pieces he had polished. Homer put the pieces in and started making doughnuts. After a couple dozen doughnuts were made, Homer decided to turn off the machine. But for some reason the machine wouldn't shut off. It kept making doughnuts, and more doughnuts, and even more doughnuts. What are they going to do with all of these doughnuts?

List as many ways as you can think of to get rid of the doughnuts. How will your ideas work?

Problem: The doughnut machine is making more doughnuts than they know what to do with. How are they going to get rid of them?

Solution	How will it work?

From your list above, circle the solution that will be the most likely to work. Will it solve the problem?

Henry and the Clubhouse

by Beverly Cleary

Henry Huggins delivers newspapers after school and on Saturdays, so he doesn't have much time to work on his clubhouse. He even has less time because Ramona Quimby always tags along on his route and makes trouble. Ramona is a terror! She always thinks up something to bother Henry about.

With a pest like Ramona around, Henry and his friends decide on a radical course of action. They post a sign on their clubhouse: "No Girls Allowed." But Ramona won't be kept out....

Advice Sheet

1. _____

_____

2. _____

_____

3. _____

_____

4. _____

_____

5. _____

6. _____

_____

7. _____

_____

8. _____

_____

9. _____

How to Build and Operate a Clubhouse

From the list below, choose the advice that you think Henry Huggins would give to clubhouse builders. Write them on the lines in the "Advice Sheet" on the left. Add any other advice that you think they might approve of.

a) Do not allow girls to join the club.
b) Buy a padlock for the door and hide the keys.
c) Make plenty of "No Girls Allowed" signs.
d) Don't throw the newspaper into the garden.
e) Have a secret clubhouse password.
f) Look for old scraps of materials from torn down houses or ones being built.
g) Keep secrets to club members ONLY.
h) Ask for a dog for your birthday.
i) Do not have a job if you want to build a clubhouse.

Henry Reed and Henry Huggins

Below is a list of things done by either Henry Reed or Henry Huggins. Place a check (√) under the name of the person who would most likely do this.

	Henry Reed	Henry Huggins
1. Had a paper route	_____	_____
2. You can't build a club-		

house when you have a
job.

3. Wrote a journal of his
experiences.

4. Started a baby-sitting
service.

5. His dog won first place
in the dog show.

6. Invented a medium size
balloon.

The Giant

by William Pène DuBois

His name is El Muchacho. He was born eight and a
half years ago. His first few days he grew very rapidly.
He multiplied three times in size the first week of his life.
At two years old he was 7 feet 2 inches tall.

How would you live if you were a giant and bigger than
the ordinary person? Describe where you would live and what
kind of life you would live.

Peter Potts

by Clifford Hicks

Peter Potts is from a small midwestern town by the
name of Fairfield. Peter has a talent for getting into trouble
purely by accident. He knew how to make April Fools of
practically everyone in town. But his ideas often backfire.

Below, in the column on the left, is a list of actions--
things done by Peter and his friend Joey. In the circles on
the right, are reactions to each of the actions done. Draw a
line from the action done to the reaction given to it.

1. Loose tooth!

2. Having a nature study at
   school. An insect house
   was almost as good as
   insects.

3. The best birthday present
   ever. Impressive and
   wouldn't cost a cent!

Beet Spilvile In Spelbound

The biggest spider web
you ever saw--all
tied together and to
the desks. Then
... A Fire Drill!!

A chicken isn't the easi-
est thing in the world
to catch.

4. April Fools Day. Boy will she be fooled!

5. One of the best spellers in the state.

6. World's Biggest Wedding Reception.

The radiator made it like spring. All of a sudden it was as though they woke from a sound sleep.

The pigeons swooped down on the corn and sponge cake like a thousand jet dive-bombers.

Clogged the washing machine, burned Joey's finger, and it rained on all the clothes.

How to Eat Fried Worms

by Thomas Rockwell

Billy has a dare and a $50 bet. He has to eat fifteen worms in fifteen days. They are fried, boiled, and smothered with catsup, horseradish, and other toppings.

Below, you are going to make a menu. The main course of your meal is going to be worms. Make a meal sound delicious enough to eat. Include in your menu a vegetable, potato, and dessert, and anything else that will go with your main dish.

AUTHOR STUDIES

While categories of books (mysteries, humor, adventure, realistic fiction) are ideal for promoting productive and critical thinking skills, a study of the books of a single author can serve equally well.

Selected works of four authors are included here to demonstrate how sharing the books of a particular author can enhance one or more areas of thinking skill development.

The variety of approaches to book illustration employed by author/artist Marcia Brown can serve as inspiration for aspiring young artists who need reassurance that no one way is best to express an idea.

Jean George's keen sense of observation combined with her ability to use vivid description should open new worlds for young readers and encourage them to sharpen observation skills.

The fluent and flexible thinking of Daniel Manus Pinkwater will convince the gifted child that imagination has no limits and stimulate his or her own productive thinking.

Finally, in both her picture books and junior novels, Jean Merrill meets a major requirement of books for the gifted. Her young readers are often left with as many questions as answers and are challenged to use their critical thinking skills in new ways.

Many fine authors are writing and illustrating for children today. The works of the best among them do not hold up a mirror image of life as the child knows it but challenge the child to go beyond his or her current level of understanding. The choices are more than could ever be shared and are waiting for discovery by eager young minds.

1. The Many Ways of Sharing the Books of Marcia Brown

Many words describe Marcia Brown: author, artist, illustrator, teacher, storyteller, puppeteer, musician, seamstress, world traveler, nature photographer and poet. Through her books she shares each of these talents and interests, inspiring her young readers to create their own unique ways to share literature.

From making rare books, to puppets, to flannel board figures, murals and diaramas, the many tales which this author/artist brings alive are ideal for sharing again and again.

ALL BUTTERFLIES (an ABC Book). Charles Scribner's Sons, 1974.

This book presents another way of looking at the 26

letters of our alphabet. Using the woodcut technique similar
to that in Once a Mouse and How, Hippo! the artist pairs the
letters and words in a very simple and imaginative way,
creating a rich visual experience in seriation.

    Activity: Have the class make a "rare" book. What
class of children would not want to create its own beautiful
alphabet book for an addition to the "Rare Book Shelf" that
can be found in many good school libraries? If you are lucky
enough to have 26 students you can assign a letter per child.
If you don't have that many, omit X, Z, and Q, which might
be difficult to find. The subject for the book might be ani-
mals--student researchers must use the natural habitat for
the background. A beautiful book could be made using flowers
for the subject. Younger children could use pictures from
seed catalogues or magazines. Higher level classes might do
"Trees"--ash, birch, catalpa, dogwood, etc., including full
drawings for each tree plus a left print. Don't forget the
name of the tree to go along with each illustration. One person could do the lettering so that it would be uniform. Be
sure that one page of the book contains all the authors' names.
The pages can be laminated and put together with metal rings.
                    (Research, Originality, Elaboration)

THE BUN (A Tale from Russia). Harcourt Brace Jova-
    novich, 1972. (K-3)

    Undoubtedly world traveler Marcia Brown once heard
children sing the song that the Bun sings over and over again
in his travels through the forest. As you read this folktale
to even the youngest children, encourage them to sing it with
you: "I was scraped from the trough, I was swept from the
bin, I was kneaded with cream, I was browned in a pan. By
the window I cooled; And had them both fooled..." The
artist's full-color pictures certainly capture the mood of the
Bun and each of its hungry pursuers. It evades the old
couple, the rabbit, the wolf, the bear--but the cunning fox
brings the story to an abrupt end. This is a charming and
delightful way to reinforce the concept of seriation.

    Activity: Children may want to try their luck at making
a Bun. Here is an easy Batter Bread recipe. (Note: The
buns will be ready to serve two hours after being started.
Since it is a batter (thinner than a dough) it rises more quickly. The batter is poured into muffin tins--it is too thin to
shape.) Blend and cool to lukewarm: 1 cup milk, scalded,

3 tablespoons sugar, 1 teaspoon salt, $\frac{1}{4}$ -cup shortening. Put
in separate mixing bowl, and stir until dissolved: 1 cup
warm water, 2 packages dry yeast. Add lukewarm milk mix-
ture and stir in $4\frac{1}{2}$ cups sifted flour. Beat about 2 minutes.
Cover and let rise in a warm place until it doubles in bulk
(about 40 minutes). Stir batter down and beat again for
about $\frac{1}{2}$ -minute. Pour into greased muffin tins. Bake about
20 minutes at 375°. Ask in advance and the cafeteria staff
may allow you to bring the filled muffin tins for baking in
their ovens. Time it so that you arrive after the children
have finished eating.

CINDERELLA or THE LITTLE GLASS SLIPPER, a free
translation from the French of Charles Perrault. Charles
Scribner's Sons, 1954. (K-5).

Handed down by word of mouth for centuries, folktales were among the first types of literature to be printed.
In France, Charles Perrault recorded eight fairy tales for
adults; Puss In Boots, and Cinderella were included. Folk-
lorists analyze folktales according to motifs or patterns.
Scholars have found versions of Cinderella in ancient Egypt,
in China in the ninth century, and in Iceland in the tenth century. Still today we find Cinderella being told and retold,
some versions more appealing than others. Without a doubt
Marcia Brown's translation is a favorite.

Activity: Point of view: challenge students to retell
the story from the point of view of the stepmother or stepsisters. How will the story change?
(Analysis, Originality, Elaboration)

DICK WHITTINGTON AND HIS CAT (folktale). Charles Scribner's Sons, 1950. (K-4)

Picture book readers enjoy a variety of media in the
illustrations. Since the purpose of an illustration is to re-
flect, interpret, and extend the text of the book, the artist
must make a considered choice as to the particular medium
of art which will best enhance the theme of the book. The
simple, direct story of Dick Whittington and His Cat is illustrated with linoleum block prints, which give a finer line
than woodcuts. In her acceptance speech for the Caldecott
Award for Cinderella, Marcia Brown tells how she selected
the color combination for a picture book: "Gold of the sum-

mer fields, gold for a small boy's thatch of hair, gold of his
dream of London, and sunrise when he heard his destiny ring
out in Bow Bells, gold of his treasure and of the chain of his
office of Lord Mayor--gold was the color for Dick Whittington. "
(Boston: Horn Book, 1957, p. 274.)

    Activity: Paint prints can be created by even the
youngest "artist. " Woodcuts and linoleum block printing can
be done by any student who is capable of handling the carving
tools. Inner-tubing cut in shapes, mounted on a wood block,
or cork mounted on wood is perhaps easier to use. The
younger students can handle a sponge cut irregularly or a
potato sliced flat, then carved. The youngest student can do
"gadget printing"--bottle cap, fork, potato masker, etc. Pour
a small amount of thick tempera in a large lid or pie tin.
Dip the block into the paint and then place it firmly on the
paper to be printed. Repeat until the paint is used up; then
dip the block in the paint again. Prints can be used to
decorate greeting cards, personal stationery (a monogram or
flower), book covers, or wrapping paper.   (Originality)

THE FLYING CARPET (retold from Richard Burton's transla-
    tion of ARABIAN NIGHTS). Charles Scribner's Sons, 1956.
    (1-5)

    Of all the forms of transportation the most marvelous
is the Flying Carpet! This wonderful age-old tale is an
exercise in evaluation as well as pure entertainment from beginning to end. Three princes, Husayn, Ali, Ahmad, sons
of the Sultan of India, were all in love with the Princess
Nur-al Nihar, their father's niece and ward. To determine
who should be the bride-groom, the sultan sent them out to
find the most extraordinary things they could. Whoever
brought back the rarest object would win the hand of the
princess. Husayn found a magic carpet which would transport
him wherever he wished. Ali found an ivory tube which would
show anything he wished to see. Ahmad found a rare magical
apple, the odor of which would cure any illness. The three
princes met before they journeyed home. As they displayed
their gifts, Husayn, looking through the tube, saw the princess
apparently at the point of death. They all jumped on the magic
carpet and were whisked to her apartment, where Ahmad used
his magic apple to revive her. The sultan could not determine
which article was the most unusual, for all had been useful in
effecting the princess' recovery. He suggested an archery
contest. Prince Ali shot farther than Husayn, but Ahmad's

arrow could not be found. The sultan decided in favor of Ali. Husayn became a hermit. Ahmad's arrow was found by the fairy Peri-banu, who pleased him so much that he married her. But this is another story...

Activity (primary): (1) Discuss with the children the idea of magic--the art by which people are said to be able to do things that are beyond the normal powers of man. Talk about mysterious effects produced by tricks, usually as entertainment: the magician pulling the rabbit out of the hat, etc. Perhaps you can locate someone in the community who would come in to do a performance for the children. (2) Bring a brightly colored "rag" rug from home. Sit on it as you read or tell the wonderful Flying Carpet story. The children will love sitting in a cluster on and around the rug. Afterwards, encourage children to write stories of magic to read or tell. This sharing should, of course, be done from the "magic rug."

Activity (intermediate): Impress the students with the fact that the author had to do much research for this picture book version of a long and complicated tale. Traditionally there were a thousand and one stories told by Scheherazade to her emperor-husband, but in existing manuscripts the tales are not always the same. The Arabian Nights' Entertainments is the title usually used in English to designate a group of tales more properly called the Thousand and One Nights. These stories, adapted and formalized by storytellers, had their origins in many lands throughout the East and were handed down by word of mouth for hundreds of years. Those most frequently reprinted have become minor classics of the world's literature. After reading The Flying Carpet ask the students to research other Arabian Nights tales. They will find "Ali Baba and the Forty Thieves," the "History of Aladdin or The Wonderful Lamp" and many others to be very entertaining. To keep the art of story telling alive, allow the best "story tellers" to ask former teachers if they can come to tell one or another of the stories to another class. To be more effective the "story teller" might tell his story dressed in an appropriate costume of the period and take along his wonderful lamp.   (Elaboration)

THE LITTLE CAROUSEL. Charles Scribner's Sons, 1946. (K-2)

When the author/artist went to New York City she lived

on the same Sullivan Street that is in The Little Carousel.
The children in this charming picture book could be on any
busy street in any large city.   They are doing universal
things: flying kites, tossing bottle caps and pennies against
the buildings, playing house--doll clothes on the railing of the
fire escape.   The clang of a cowbell on the pushcart with
fresh clams could just as likely be the ice cream truck that
pays regular visits to every sub-division and neighborhood.
Suddenly, another sound, thin high music!   Anthony and all
the other children discover the merry-go-round.   The children took ride after ride--all except Anthony.   The children
will be delighted at the way Mr. Corelli solves Anthony's
problem, which finally allows him to have the longest ride
of all!

        Activity: Allow the children to work in small groups,
constructing their own carousels.   They won't need the red
wagon or the black and white horse because their merry-go-
round will whirl around on the turntable of the record player
(16 rpm is ideal speed, 33 rpm is "top speed").   The base
will be a large circle of cardboard--and don't forget the hole
in the middle.   The horses, lions and elephants can be created
out of papier-maché.   Pipe-cleaner figures are fun and easy
to make.   Malt straws can hold up the red and yellow canopy.
Finally, have try-outs for the readers who will tape the story.
Don't forget the sound effects (bell for the pushcart peddler
and the wonderful carousel music).   (Originality, Elaboration)

THE NEIGHBORS.   Charles Scribner's Sons, 1967.   (K-1)

        Both animals and people trick their friends and neigh-
bors in folk literature.   The plot of this Russian animal tale
involves a conflict to be resolved through several episodes.
Repetition is a basic element in many folktale plots.   Frequently, three is the magic number for building suspense.
In this one, three animals (wolf, bear, cock) offer assistance
to the hare, who has lost his house to the fox.   Repetition of
responses is also frequently a part of the structure.   The fox
calls out to each animal, "If I jump out you'd better watch
out.   The fur will fly when I do come out!"   But as the hare
explains the situation to cock, the cock succeeds in scaring
the fox out and then moves in with hare to become his new
friend.   This is a delightful book to share to the point where
the problem is defined.   Children can then brainstorm for
the best solution.

Creative Activity: "Ice Houses"

Objective: The fox's house of ice melted quickly in
the warm spring sun. The children can use the idea as a
basis for a science lesson. Measuring, timing, estimating
and averaging are usually not fun, but when done with an ice
cube they can be a new experience for all.
Materials: Ice cubes, paper cups, paper towels, clock
graph paper, colored pencils or pens.

1. We all know ice melts faster in the warm sunshine than
in the shade, but how much faster? Let's estimate how long
it will take an ice cube to melt if left in the refrigerator,
not the freezer; how long it will take for an ice cube to melt
sitting on a desk in the classroom, not in sunshine; and how
long it would take if the ice cube were placed on a window
sill in the sunshine. The ice cubes will each be in a paper
cup.

2. Record your estimates on your graph.

3. Place one ice cube in a paper cup and place it in a refrigerator. Mark on the cup the time it was placed in there
and check on it occasionally. Place one ice cube in a paper
cup and set it on the science table, not in the sun. Write
the time on the cup. Place one ice cube in a paper cup and
set it in the sun. Write the time on the cup.

4. While the children are waiting to see some progress they
can compare estimates, average the class guesses for each
of the three cubes, and see how close their own estimates are
to the class averages. How much difference was there in
each category?

5. When all the ice is melted in each cup the children will
compute the length of time it took, record it on their charts
and see how close their estimates were and how close the
class averages were. The refrigerator test may need to be
done at home.

PUSS IN BOOTS, a free translation from the French of Charles
    Perrault. Charles Scribner's Sons. (K-4)

The third son of a miller lamented the fact that he in-
herited only a cat. He considered eating the cat and making
a muff from its skin. To save himself--and help his master--

the cat asked for a sack and a pair of boots. The sly rogue snared a rabbit and two partridges with the sack. These gifts earned the king's friendship. In the meantime Puss tells his master that his fortune is made if he will just follow his advice. Just as the king and his daughter were passing, the cat feigned that his master was drowning. Naturally, the guards saved him. Since the cat had hidden his clothes, the officers of the king's wardrobe had to fetch some of his handsome clothes for the "Marquis of Carabas." The king would have nothing but that the Marquis ride with them in the carriage. (The cat's scheme was working!!) Dashing ahead of the royal carriage, the cat told the peasants to say the land belonged to the Marquis of Carabas or he would make mincemeat of them. Reaching a great castle, he tricked the ogre into changing into a mouse, which he promptly ate. The castle became his master's and Puss became a great lord-- the dashing hero in boots and plumed hat.

Creative Activities: Productive Thinking

1. a) List a minimum of twenty-five folk tale heroes (human or animal). Number your list.
   b) List a minimum of twenty-five folk tale villains. Number your list.
   c) Select two numbers from a box containing numbers from one to twenty-five. The first number selected matches the name with that number on the hero list. The second number matches the name with that number on the villain list.
   d) Compose a message from the hero to the villain which is logical and reveals something about each.
   Example: Puss-in-Boots to Rumpelstiltskin: "Don't bother to stop by, my master's new wife already knows how to spin straw into gold."

2. Different forms of story introductions could be listed by middle-grade students. Remind them that Puss in Boots starts with the familiar "Once upon a time there was..." They will be eager to get to the library to find many other "Long, long ago...," "Once there lived...," "Many seasons ago...," etc. Even the reluctant student who thinks he/she is past "easy books" will find renewed interest in this assignment and will no longer feel restricted to "bigger books," realizing, one hopes, that one never gets too old for "picture books." (Fluency)

THE SNOW QUEEN by Hans Christian Andersen. Translated
from the Danish text by R. P. Keigwin. Charles Scribner's
Sons, 1972. (1-5)

Andersen was not afraid to show children cruelty,
morbidity, sorrow, or even death. In this long tale, The
Snow Queen, a glass splinter enters Kay's eye and stabs his
heart, which becomes cold as ice. The splinter came from
the mirror of a wicked imp. The mirror reflected everything
good as trivial and everything bad as monstrous. The imps
flew up to heaven with the mirror. It fell out of their hands
and splintered as it hit the earth. Kay then became spiteful
and angry with Gerda, his former friend and neighbor. As
bold boys often do, Kay tied his toboggan to the back of a
sleigh--this one painted dead white. Suddenly the horses
galloped out of town and, try as he might, Kay could not
free his sled. The driver was the Snow Queen. Gerda was
hurt by the changed behavior of Kay but, still loving him,
she searched for him. She went to the garden of an old, old
woman but the flowers knew only their own stories. She met
a crow who led her to a prince and princess, but they had not
heard of Kay. They gave her boots and a muff, and a golden
coach to ride in when they sent her on her way. Robbers
stopped the golden coach. At the insistence of a little robber
girl, Gerda was left alive. Some wood pigeons said that Kay
had gone with the Snow Queen to Lapland. The reindeer de-
livered her there and the Lapp and Finn women gave Gerda
directions to the Snow Queen's palace. When Gerda found Kay,
her tears melted the piece of mirror out of his heart. Weep-
ing the splinter from his eye, Kay realized what a vast and
empty place the Snow Queen's palace was. Gerda led Kay out
of the snow palace and Spring met them on their way home.
When they reached grandmother's door they realized that they
were now grown-up--but still children at heart.

Activities: (1) Box movie. A simple box movie may
be constructed by attaching dowel rods at either side of a suit
box or carton. Strips of shelf paper may be used to illustrate
the sequence of events in The Snow Queen. This story is
ideal for a class project--dividing the class into smaller
groups and assigning one part of the story to each group, and
finally putting the parts together with masking tape for a "full
length movie." One child can roll the paper by turning the
rod as the narrator relates the story to the group, or the
story can be taped so that one child can listen and manipulate
the movie at the same time. (2) The same principle can be
carried out with children who wish to make individual "movies."

Drawings or pictures in a series may be made on a strip of adding-machine tape and pulled through slits cut in an envelope. (3) To focus on just part of the long tale, a child or children might do a flower collage for Part Three, the flower garden of the woman who could do magic. Flower and garden magazines and seed catalogues will produce all the flowers needed. To be sure that it is a Snow Queen flower garden, have the children list the names of the flowers in Part Three: blue violets, roses, tiger lilies, convolvulus (they'll have to look that one up), etc. before they start searching for flowers.

(Elaboration, Originality)

THE STEADFAST TIN SOLDIER. Text by Hans Christian Andersen. Translated by M. R. James. Charles Scribner's Sons, 1953. (K-5)

Two of Andersen's tales are said to be autobiographical, The Ugly Duckling and The Steadfast Tin Soldier. The sad tale of the painfully shy but loyal tin soldier and his love for the cold and unbending toy ballerina is said by some authorities to represent Andersen's rejection by the woman he loved. Many of Andersen's stories have been beautifully illustrated in single editions, and some of the best are done by Marcia Brown.

A little boy had a set of 25 tin soldiers made out of the same tin spoon. Since there was not quite enough tin left, one soldier had only one leg, but he stood as solidly as the rest, gazing longingly at a paper dancer who wore a gauze dress. One day the little soldier fell from the window sill to the ground three stories below, where he was found by several boys. They made a boat for him from newspaper and sailed him in the gutter which emptied into a canal. There he was swallowed by a fish, the fish was caught, sold at the market, and the Tin Soldier ended up in the kitchen of the house where he had been before. Soon he was back on the table looking at the dancer. For no reason the boy threw him into the fire, and a sudden draft whisked the dancer off the table into the stove with the Tin Soldier. When the maid took out the ashes the next day, she found him in the shape of a little tin heart, and all that was left of the dancer was her spangle, burned black as coal.

Activity: Diorama. A two-section diorama can be constructed so that when the final event is told, the box can be turned to reveal the last scene. More than likely the children will choose to do the scene where the Tin Soldier sees the lovely paper castle. In front of it little trees stand around a lake (use a mirror) with swans made of wax or papier maché. A beautiful ballerina can be made with pipe cleaners, gauze, and a blue ribbon (don't forget that gold spangle). The Tin Soldier can be made by covering a tall, thin vanilla-flavoring bottle with red and blue construction paper. The towering black hat and rifle that he held tighter than ever on that boat ride will complete his costume. The second section will contain the little tin heart and a burned spangle surrounded by ashes.

Box sculpture. Get an assortment of cardboard containers (oatmeal boxes, hat boxes, jewelry boxes and boxes that held canned vegetables at the supermarket). You will also need miscellaneous materials such as colored paper, ribbon, string and big buttons. Supplies will include glue or tape, scissors and tempera paint and brush. You'll need lots of red and blue along with black and white paint. Containers such as those suggested above, when combined with other materials, lend themselves to the construction of a life-size Tin Soldier. Individual "Tin Soldiers" can be made by the children using plastic liquid soap containers for the base shape. (Elaboration)

STONE SOUP (An Old Tale). Charles Scribner's Sons, 1947. (K-2)

The number of folk tales published as single books and illustrated as picture books has increased tremendously since Wanda Gág's Snow White and the Seven Dwarfs appeared in 1938. It was Marcia Brown who developed the trend to illustrate single tales when her Stone Soup was published in 1947.

Three soldiers trick an entire village into providing ingredients for their soup. At first the villagers hid their foodstuffs, but clever soldiers conned them into sharing by nonchalantly setting to work making their own Stone Soup. By the end of the tale the curious villagers had supplied a huge black kettle, salt and pepper, and numerous other ingredients to accompany three large, round, smooth stones in the water-filled pot. Double-page spreads are used as if to emphasize the greatness of the project!

Activity (primary): The storytelling of Stone Soup may be varied by using a flannel or felt board. This is a cumulative tale (one in which elements are added), providing

reinforcement of the development of seriation. The enthusiasm
of the storyteller will capture the children's attention in the
first telling and, before long, even very young children will
help tell the story by adding figures and ingredients to that
hugh Stone Soup pot. (Seriation)

Activity (intermediate): To cultivate and continue interest in the so-called "easy picture books, " do a study with
the students comparing different artists' styles. Comparing
books with the same theme or subject can be interesting and
help in understanding different art techniques. Stone Soup
may be compared with Zemach's Nail Soup. A hungry soldier
obtains food by creating "Nail Soup" in a Yugoslavian folk
tale. Placing a nail in water, he asks for vegetables to give
it flavor. In Stone Soup, three soldiers trick an entire village
into providing ingredients for their soup. The students will
also read real meaning into the story that younger children
may miss. (Analysis)

TAMARINDO! Charles Scribner's Sons, 1960.

Many picture storybooks, particularly Marcia Brown's,
provide familiarity with cultures in all parts of the world.
A donkey is lost--a very serious matter in Sicily. Four little
boys who are sure they can catch the frisky animal follow
him down to the sea. Here the story turns from serious to
amusing when the boys are detracted from their purpose and
decide to go "skinny dipping. " A herd of goats steals their
clothes. Will they catch the donkey? More important, will
they catch the goats and retrieve their clothes? Children will
enjoy forecasting the outcome of the boy's predicament!

Activity: To help make that which is foreign seem
familiar, ask: Why was a lost donkey such a serious matter?
Children may say that a donkey is used to carry olives to
the olive press, grapes to the wine press, beans to the house,
because it says so in Tamarindo! What is a wine press?
Keep posing questions to develop a full-blown research project
on that large island in the Mediterranean Sea (Sicily). Discuss: topography, climate, economic life, history, etc.
(Analysis, Research)

THE WILD SWANS. Text by Hans Christian Andersen.
Translated by M. R. James. Charles Scribner's Sons,
1963. (1-5)

Hans Christian Andersen is generally credited with being the first author of modern fairy tales, although some of his stories, such as The Wild Swans, are definite adaptions of old folk tales. (Compare Andersen's The Wild Swans with Grimm's The Seven Ravens, for example.) Every Andersen story bears his unmistakable stamp of gentleness, melancholy, and faith in God. Even his adaptations of old tales contain deeper hidden meanings, making them very much his own. In this version, the artist has captured the mystical beauty of The Wild Swans with her pen and wash drawings in black and gray tones, with the slightest touch of coral for warmth.

There lived a King who had eleven sons and one daughter, Elisa. Their mother died and the King married a woman who turned the boys out of the palace, transforming them into eleven beautiful wild swans. Elisa was boarded in the country with some laborers. The plot weaves many episodes related to the quiet, gentle weaving that Elisa does for her brothers' shirts. The melancholy mood of the whole tale turns to absolute joy as Elisa throws the shirts over the swans, creating once again the human forms of her eleven brothers.

Activity: A mural. After discussing the scenes and characters to be portrayed, each child may make a sketch of one part, or small groups may meet to plan one section. A variety of material can be used. Crayon drawings can be cut out, pinned in place, and then glued to a large sheet of wrapping paper. This type of assembled mural is made easily and quickly. Chalk or tempera paint is also effective. A mural of paper sculpture creates an interesting three-dimensional effect when the figures or objects are fastened to the mural with small rolls of masking tape.

(Originality, Elaboration)

2.   Visual Communication with the Books of Jean George

Our brightest children are often limited in their search for knowledge by the environment which surrounds them. Urban children in particular have few opportunities to discover the many wonders of nature, particularly those of the ocean, forest or desert.

In both her picture books and junior novels, Jean George brings alive for the younger reader worlds of nature stretching from the Alaskan tundra to the depths of the ocean. In vivid detail she shares her own feeling of oneness with nature, from the thrills of shooting the murky rapids of the Potomac on a sycamore log to the quiet hours spent on the floor of a forest inspecting the insects, the moss, or observing a colorful bird.

In contrast to television's concern with a large single image, Jean George takes children on a visual tour of worlds within worlds. Every child, and particularly that child with an insistently questioning mind should have the opportunity to explore the worlds of nature as seen through this talented author's eyes.

BEASTLY INVENTIONS. David McKay Co., 1970.

The variety of adaptations that the animal kingdom must make to its environment is fascinatingly revealed in this book. Included as well is a collection of the "exceptions" to the rule: animals that grow and thrive on metal, animals that produce a glue that man cannot duplicate, and animals that produce music heard over great distances by sea creatures. The author envisions the day when man will be able to communicate with wild creatures in their own language.

Shown are the wonders of sponges and how they can be broken into pieces and yet return to their original shape within a twenty-four-hour period. The bees act as one body in the hive rather than as individuals, and when an emergency or need arises, take on jobs for which they are apparently unqualified.

The author also explores the ingenuity of many creatures in fulfilling their need to travel. The hydra turns cart wheels; the springrail, a tiny creature less than one-sixteenth of an inch long, vaults two or three feet in the air. The starfish uses a hydraulic system to travel. The boa defies gravity to move from branch to branch.

The sex habits of the lower forms of animals, especially the arachnids, have been developed to assure the continuation of the species even though the act is a precarious and sometimes fatal one for the male.

Homes of animals have been invented to suit particular needs. Insubstantial homes are built but very complex layouts are contrived and built too. Parenting of youngsters sometimes reveals unusual aspects, but serves the purpose of propagation of the species. Strange food-gathering habits of some animals defy the imagination of man.

Some animals have over-developed certain senses to aid them in their adaptations. A group of lower animals has developed an awareness of the lethal X-ray that sends them away from the rays. Temperature is one of the stimuli which sends birds on migration. Night fliers use stars as guides; day fliers use the sun. Wind is also a factor in bird migration.

Other topics covered in this awesome collection of animal behaviors include hibernation, camouflage, and the ways in which some species have adapted to live with man. Cockroaches have been provided a veritable tropical isle by man. Moths have changed colors through generations to adapt to city environment.

The author suggests that even the human animals change, and perhaps someday we will have figured out everything the animal knows. Our minds will know to recoil from strontium-90. We will have driven away pests with their own chemicals and signals. Perhaps our intelligence will match the instincts of lower forms of life and we will not have to drive wild things into extinction or rationalize our social disasters. What mind boggling concepts to challenge the gifted child!

Discussion

What are some things that you must do each day to adapt to your environment? (Fluency)

Do you always react to things with a thought-out plan? Do you sometimes react instinctively? Do you ever react creatively? (Do you try some way that is new to adjust to a situation?) (Fluency)

Are there any things in our environment today that threaten the existence of mankind? What can man do about these things? (Fluency, Problem solving)

Creative Activities

1) Ask the children to think of just one thing in the environment which threatens man as he exists today. (Air, water, nuclear pollution, etc.) Also ask them to think of social pressures which may tend to threaten the creative processes of an individual. Discuss. (Analysis)

2) Working in groups, ask each group to decide on an animal
    which is threatened in some way by its environment.
    Write a story about this animal. Tell how the animal
    adapts or changes as it develops a <u>new</u> way to overcome
    a situation.   (Originality)

3) If the animal makes physical changes, draw a before-and-
    after picture to show the difference.   (Originality)

    As each story is read other groups may make sugges-
tions on how the character could have made different or additional changes.   (Fluency, Flexibility)

HOLE IN THE TREE. E. P. Dutton, 1957.

    Appealing to every child's curiosity about a hole in a
tree, this book leads the child to discover how some holes
become so large. The story involves two children, Scott
and Paula Gordon. The hole begins with a bark beetle which
Scott blew from his shoulder.
    The bark beetle was not a good thing to have in the
tree, for she carried with her a fungus disease that would
kill the apple tree. She laid her eggs. Then the wood borer,
another beetle, tunneled deeper into the tree and laid her eggs.
The woodpecker enlarged the hole in his search for the larva
of the beetles. The hole was large enough now for the black
bee to eat through the fungus-rotted wood and lay her eggs.
The bees inhabited the tree during the winter.
    By Spring, the hole was big enough to be enlarged for
a chickadee's nest. In the Fall a deer mouse found that this
was an excellent place for her young. The hole was enlarged again by the woodpecker, then a nuthatch, then flying
squirrels, bluebirds, a flicker, and finally by Scott, who discovered it to be an excellent place in which to hide treasures.

Discussion

1) This book is one of constant discovery. How many have
    ever watched one thing in nature to discover what happens
    to it? Have you ever watched a bird's nest from its in-
    ception to the time after it has been abandoned by the
    birds?   (Analysis)

2) Have you ever opened just one encyclopedia and gone
    through it slowly, stopping frequently to read and observe?
                                            (Visual Literacy)

3) What are some ways you have used to discover what goes on in the world around you? At home? At school? In the classroom? Is discovering a learning process? Can one go through life without a desire to discover new things? Is the process of discovery always pleasant? Does one sometimes have to readjust one's thinking during the discovery process? Give examples.

(Visual Communication)

Creative Activities

1) Have enough encyclopedias on hand so that every child will have one volume. Do not allow the children to exchange books. Tell them to start browsing. See how many different and new things they can discover.

(Fluency, Visual Literacy)

2) Have the children jot down each new thing they discover from one volume. Allow a suitable length of time. When several children are finished with their lists, suggest that they number their notes, from the least important item (to them) to the most important. (Evaluation)

3) On a sheet of drawing paper ask the children to start with a small design or circle. Print in this Note #1. Color it lightly with crayon. Make another design around the first for Note #2. Continue until all the notes are recorded on the drawing. This should make an interesting design as well as a fact sheet to reinforce learning.

(Elaboration)

HOOK A FISH, CATCH A MOUNTAIN. E. P. Dutton, 1975.

Spinner, a city girl who was interested in ballet, was expected to join in the family fishing contest. Her father expected to win the three-generation trophy in the family's "biggest catch" race. Spinner was expected to compete with seasoned fishermen of the family--her grandfather, uncle, and two young male cousins.

Spinner managed to land a trout in a very unorthodox manner. She would have abandoned the attempt, feeling empathy for FISH, if the other family members had not gathered around expecting the utmost of her.

Greatly hurt emotionally because her father insisted on having FISH mounted instead of releasing him, Spinner was ready to return to her stable, secure city life. However, Alligator, her "fishing cousin," changed her mind, suggesting a back-packing trip into the mountains to research the reason for the absence of cutthroats in a stream where they had once lived and thrived.

Their adventures are told with a genuine understanding, by a person who understands and values nature. It shows that with scientific expertise and determination one can rehabilitate the streams with their natural inhabitants.

Discussion

1) Ask if students have been trout fishing. In many state parks, fish not native to cold spring-fed streams are stocked by the Conservation Department.

2) Ask the children if they ever hear their grandparents say that they used to catch many fish in the streams in their area. Do they say that they do not catch the big ones anymore? What do you think the reason might be?
(Analysis)

3) What has the Conservation Commission done to help keep fishing alive for people today?   (Research)

4) What might happen if the environmentalists and naturalists lose interest in researching and protecting wildlife?
(Analysis)

5) Do you think future generations might resent our lack of concern and forethought if we ignore pollution and pro- tection problems?   (Analysis)

6) How do you think these future people might be harmed?
(Analysis)

7) Is fishing really a form of human conservation? How?
(Analysis)

Creative Activity

Fly-tying would be too difficult for younger students. The work is intricate and requires well-defined small muscle control of the fingers. However, the children could experi- ment on a larger-scale model using a pipecleaner as a pseudo hook.

Colored feathers, metallic thread, wool, fur, peacock feathers, and other odds and ends can easily be collected. Many fathers are trout fishermen and will be glad to donate left-over material. Have the children bring to school all the bits and pieces they can gather.

Give each child a pipe cleaner and have them bend the end to form a hooklike end. Let them select the materials for their giant fly.

Many will want to research trout flies. These can be reproduced. Glue will be needed to keep the materials together satisfactorily.

Have someone find a large limb. It could be fastened securely to a bulletin board or the wall, or it could stand upright in a corner by putting it in a can and encasing it in plaster of paris.

Let the children attach their fly to the limb with a light-weight fishing line.

This should make a colorful display for the drab month of March.   (Originality)

JULIE OF THE WOLVES. Awarded the 1973 Newbery Medal. Harper & Row, 1972. (Junior Novel)

Jean Craighead George shows a tender, delicate insight not only into the lives of a wolf pack, but into the life of a young Eskimo girl who must become independent and finally concede to giving up the simple life which she understands.

Julie, or Miyax in Eskimo, is seen through the death of her mother by Kapugen, her independent father. He leaves the city life and takes Julie to share with him the life of a seal hunter. Here she grows and learns nature's ways until her ordered life is interrupted by an aunt who insists that the girl should go to school. Julie has to leave her father and live with the aunt.

She adjusts to this life and then hears about her father's apparent death while on a seal hunt.

Buoyed by letters from a pen pal, Amy, who lives in California, Julie longs to see San Francisco. When the city situation worsens, Julie decides to marry the son of her father's friend, Naka. The marriage has been prearranged according to the old Eskimo customs.

When Julie encounters this dull-witted boy, she is alarmed, but his mother says they will only be brother and sister. However, Daniel, teased by the village boys, tries to take advantage of Julie. She packs a few belongings and leaves, heading for San Francisco and Amy's alluring life.

Miyax loses her sense of direction. It is summer and the North Star cannot guide her to the airport city. She becomes so hungry that she decides to become part of a wolf pack. Learning the wolves' ways, she is accepted by Amaroq, the leader. He sees that she is fed, and she survives the winter, becoming a part of the wolf pack.

When Miyax once again encounters civilization she finds that changes are occurring in Alaska. She too must change.

The story ends with the same determination with which it began. One wonders if Julie is really making a happy decision as she "pointed her boots toward Kapugen" and the new life which awaits her.

Discussion

1) What do you think about Kapugen's advice to Julie, that when she was afraid she should do something else? How might this advice be helpful? (Analysis)

2) If you were lost in a forest, what are some of the things you might need to help you survive? Would knowledge of the wildlife in that place be useful? Why? Would you need any tools? How could you shelter and feed yourself? How could you make a fire? (Fluency, Problem solving)

3) Did you notice the color images that surrounded Julie's early childhood? What colors do you associate with an important event in your life? (Visual Communication)

4) Have you ever made up new words to a song to keep yourself occupied as Julie did? Just for fun?
(Fluency, Originality)

Creative Activity

List some of the color images that Jean George presents in the second part of the book:

- rosy-gray house on the outside -
- gold brown inside -
- black kayak -
- dark gold and soft brown were the old men -
- ocean was green and white and rimmed with fur of Kapugen's hood -
- the black, purple, blue, fire-red of the Bladder Feast -

- Kapugen's hand was rose-colored -
- the old woman's (Shaman's) face streaked with
    black soot -
- the bent woman seemed all violet-colored that
    night -
- flickering yellow as the old men beat their drums
    round Kapugen's stove -
- silver memory, the day when the sun comes
    over the horizon for the first time in the
    winter -
- murky tan while fishing with Kapugen -
- metallic silver-gold of the sealskin -
- Naka's eyes were dark and shining -

Give each child a sheet of white drawing paper. Tell them to put a dot in the center of the paper. Then mark one-inch spaces around the outside of the sheet. Using a ruler, lightly draw connecting lines from the outside marks to the central dot.

Using one crayon only, see how many shades of your "experience color" you can make. One shade in each triangle. Some children will be able to develop as many as ten or more shades while others may not be able to produce more than three or four. Continue around the page, repeating the shades from lightest to darkest.

When finished, ask the children to cut a silhouette from black paper to depict the event they wish to represent.
(Visual Communication)

THE MOON OF THE GRAY WOLVES. Thomas Y. Crowell, 1969.

Toklat Pass in Mount Sheldon, Alaska was cold and snow-filled at four on an afternoon in November. This barrenness and cold did not deter the black wolf as he watched the caribou entering the pass as they migrated from the foot of Mt. McKinley to the Sanctuary River. He knew that food would be plentiful for his pack.

Since May, his pack had worked individually or in pairs while the job of parenting the young pups took precedence and the wolves remained homebound. Now, with the cold of Autumn air, something triggered the black wolf to lead his pack on the hundred-mile trail to Sanctuary River.

The first hunt this year is for an ailing caribou buck. As the older members of the pack move in for the kill, a lanky pup dashes in to help his father. This results in the leader being flipped and stunned by the caribou. However, the kill is accomplished. The pack is fed. The magpies, ravens, and eagles fly in to feed on the remains.

Discussion

What evidence do you find in the behavior of the wolves of traits generally attributed to humans? Loyalty, affection, responsibility?   (Analysis)

Creative Activity

Students can create a puppet show with speaking and action parts.

Let students decide which characters they would like to portray. Cut silhouettes about 14"-16" for the black wolf and the other adult wolves, larger for the caribou, smaller for the pups and birds. Many characters can be portrayed-- the owls, ravens, magpies, ptarmigan, moose and her calf, etc. Authentic reproductions requiring research should be stressed.

Cut off one part of each animal. (Head of the black wolf, the tail of his mate, the paw of another, etc.). Attach the body part of the animal to a straight stick or thin dowel with a needle and thread. Two or three stitches should be enough. Then attach the "cut-off" portion to another stick. Both sticks are held in one hand when the animal is not talking. When the animal talks, move the sticks slightly up and down to set it off from the other animals.

Stress that students should portray the interdependence of these creatures.

This should be enacted with the chalkledge as the stage. The artists can draw the background of the tundra on the board to serve as a backdrop.

Invite another class to enjoy The Moon of the Gray Wolves.

THE MOON OF THE SALAMANDERS. Thomas Y. Crowell, 1967.

Instinctively, an old male salamander lumbers out of his home in a Michigan forest toward the spring pond. On only one night of the year, during the first spring rain after the first spring thaw, the salamanders mate just as their ancestors did millions of years ago.

The slow-moving salamander meets other woodland creatures on his journey to his mating dance. A woodsnail unlocking his thirteen doors, a moth that has just been freed from his cocoon, the spring flowers, a worm in an acorn are all responding to the call of spring.

Upon reaching the pond, the salamander chooses a female and dances the ritual of fertilization. Leaving a buttonlike spermatophore on a leaf, the salamander returns home. The female carries on the ritual and returns to the pond the next night to lay her eggs in a jellylike substance on a twig. She leaves her eggs to be mothered by the pond.

After this mating, other creatures begin their ritual for reproduction.

As spring continues, the salamander wakens again from his deep sleep to enter the woodland for another year of life--a repetition of his species for the last three hundred million years.

Discussion

Have you ever observed a creature in the woods? Describe it. What color was it? How did it move? What kind of eyes did it have? What did it eat?

(Visual Communication)

Creative Activities

1) Each child selects a creature that he has observed, either in his own yard or neighborhood or in the forests.

   From the encyclopedia and other reference books, find out about this creature--where it lives, what it eats, whether or not it hibernates. (Research)

2) Pretend that you are the creature. Write an autobiography. Describe yourself and a day in your life.

   Share your autobiography with your classmates. Each reads his story. (Originality, Elaboration)

3) Visualize the classroom as a woodland. Each child acts out a typical day. Remember that some creatures are the prey of others along the food chain.

   Each child could tag the child who would be his prey. That child sits down. See who is left standing.

   (Elaboration)

4) Language Activity: Noun Phrases
  A noun phrase consists of a noun plus its adjective
modifier or modifiers.
  One kind of adjective points out or limits a noun in
some way. These are determiners or noun markers such
as: the, some, that, one, many, his, etc. Another
kind of adjective describes or limits the noun.
  Under the noun, write the adjective that describes the
noun. Add your own determiner (noun marker) and make
a noun phrase.

SALAMANDER   FERN   SHRIMP

_____   _____   _____

_____   _____   _____

_____   _____   _____

WOODPECKER   SQUIRREL   WOODSNAIL

_____   _____   _____

_____   _____   _____

_____   _____   _____

blue-spotted	foot-chewing	fiddlehead	thirteen-doored
downy	egg-laying	land-lumbering	live-bearing
scolding	hungry	transparent	glittering
primitive-eyed	blunt-headed	fence-setting	curly-tailed
fuzzy	chasing	soft-antennaed	clawless
		sharp-tapping	curly-leafed

MY SIDE OF THE MOUNTAIN. E. P. Dutton & Company,
  1959. (Junior Novel) Runner-up: The Newbery Medal.
  An American Library Association Notable Book; A Lewis
  Carroll Shelf Award Book; Runner-up: Hans Christian
  Andersen Award.

  Sam Gribley is holed-up in his tree home as December
begins. The first snow had fallen. He wonders how he will
get out through the snow and into the open. He had been
working since May, learning how to survive in the wilderness
of the Catskill Mountains, alone and without the help of other
humans.

The story is one that shows a young boy's desire to become independent. Sam goes all the way toward his goal. He experiences the unrelenting forces of nature and man's need to adapt to its demands. It also shows that man needs companionship: Sam begins to know and become compatible with the animals which inhabit the forest with him.

Sam grows from a young boy with a seemingly impossible dream, to a young man who has the security of knowing that he has made his dream into a reality--and has accomplished it by himself.

Discussion

1) Have you ever wanted to be completely independent? How might you become independent without leaving your own home? (Analysis)

2) Do you think that a twelve-year-old could be entirely self-sufficient? What basic needs would have to be furnished by parents or guardians? (Fluency, Analysis)

3) How many things could you do for yourself that would make you more dependent on yourself for entertainment? for healthy living conditions? For good grades? For spending money? (Fluency, Flexibility)

4) What forces or people in your environment might hamper you from achieving your independence? (Analysis)

5) Do you depend on your friends for anything? The way you dress? The entertainment you enjoy? The books you read? The grades you make in school? Are your parents the only people who stand in the way of your independence? Your teachers? Your friends? The television set? (Analysis)

Creative Activities

1) Although it appears that Sam was running away from home, he really seemed to be running toward something. He sought his independence from a world of pre-packaged luxuries.

Suggest to the children that it might be interesting to experiment with one's own amount of dependence and independence.

Just as Sam had a goal, so the children must first decide on one area in their lives where they would like to be totally dependent on themselves.

Caution the children to be realistic. Some goals they might choose would be:

1. getting up by themselves in the morning
2. doing home chores without being reminded or forced
3. keeping their bedroom in top-notch shape
4. setting a bedtime and getting to bed at that time with no prodding
5. not eating between meals
6. doing their own homework and studying for class
7. bathing and changing underclothes every day
8. making new friends, or breaking away from friends who may not be good companions for them
9. listening to instructions in class and doing their own work--trying to figure out the correct answers without constant help from classmates or teachers
10. getting along with others

Each child will probably have a different goal. Suggest that each write his or her objective on a sheet of paper and hand it to you.

Tell the children that they might think of this difficulty to be overcome as akin to Sam's need for food and water. It was a vital force that had to be met. It was a daily occurrence and had to be solved on that basis.

Have the children keep a written account of their feelings, and when they want to return to the old life. List how they invented new ways to satisfy the demands put upon them.   (Decision-making, Problem-solving)

2) It would be good to have a daily sharing period. At the end of one week, have each child write a story about his or her adventure toward independence from the notes each has kept. Share the stories with classmates. Did anyone in the class ever have to establish this type of independence in their lives? Did they have the same emotional response? Did they solve the problem in the same way?   (Originality, Evaluation)

SPRING COMES TO THE OCEAN. Thomas Y. Crowell, 1965.

On December 21, the days begin to lengthen and the trip toward Spring beings again. As the days begin to get longer, the inner mechanism of the sea creatures responds.
Sargasso weed moves to the Gulf Stream. The hermit crab runs up the cool beach in January, desperately looking for an uninhabited conch shell in which to live after he sheds his outgrown shell. He will wait here for his new skeleton to harden. The hermit attaches a sea anemone and a sponge to his new home so that his new, too pink shell will be camouflaged. He can now walk the sea floor in safety. At this time the mating of the male and female is completed and the mysterious genetic code is passed on.
Thus begins a vivid description of the teeming life beneath the ocean. In rich, descriptive language the author reveals the habitats of the sponge, the elvers, the young flounder, the green turtles, the octopus, the porpoise, the herring, the grunion and the gray whale. It is a world within a world, filled with awe and wonder to stretch young minds beyond their current levels of knowledge.

Discussion

1) You are on a scuba diving expedition. Describe what you might see. Are these creatures plants or animals?
(Fluency)

2) Can you name some other books you have read where mothers (human or animal) spend much time with their young? Have you read any books which show the opposite?   (Fluency)

3) If you were a hermit crab about ready to shed its outer skeleton, describe how you would feel.   (Originality)

4) Describe the feelings that the baby gray whale had when it could not find its mother. Describe the mother's feelings when it knew its baby was lost.   (Empathy)

Creative Activities

Working in groups of two, have students select one sea creature. Ask them to develop four body actions that might portray that creature.
For example: The Dolphin

1. Right foot forward and step (count 1)
    Left foot forward and step ahead (count 2)
    Repeat once.   Right, left.
2. Head right (standing in place)   (count 1)
    Head left (count 2)
    Repeat once.
3. Arms out at sides (count 1)
    Arms behind back (count 2)
    Repeat once.
4. With arms still behind the back and standing
    in place, Hips left (count 1)
    Hips right (count 2)
    Repeat once.

Now put all these actions together - step right then left 1, 2, 3, 4.   Head right then left 1, 2, 3, 4.   Arms to side and back 1, 2, 3, 4.   Hips to right then left - 1, 2, 3, 4.

Now put on a disco record (Disco Inferno: B. Gibb, R. Gibb, M. Gibb.   Stigwood Music, Inc. works well because the tempo is slower.)   Everyone will be surprised that these four simple movements will create a new and interesting disco dance.   Children may wish to experiment further with movements and name their dance for the sea creature they are interpreting.   (Originality, Elaboration)

Language Activity - Vocabulary Enrichment

Using a dictionary, write an appropriate definition for each of the following words used in Jean George's Spring Comes to the Ocean.

A. fluke _____
B. pigment _____
C. inaugurate _____
D. collide _____
E. carapace _____
F. voracious _____
G. phosphorescent _____
H. monarch _____
I. alkaloid _____
J. swimmerettes _____

Now fill in each blank with the appropriate word in the sentences from Spring Comes to the Ocean.   Be sure to add correct suffixes where necessary.

A. "He (the hermit crab) wiggled and moved, tensing all the muscles on his back and feet until he had pulled himself away from his old _____."

B. "He (the hermit crab) ate _____, stuffing the food into his many-parted mouth with his small claws."

C. "Here he (the hermit) threw out his _____ and stopped himself."

D. "He rolled over and slashed, for the ink was an _____ and burned his skin. It also stunned his sense of smell."

E. "The _____ jellyfish were lighting the rocks and caverns with a dull blue light."

F. "They beat up and down and spiraled her among the sponges with grace and speed, for the _____ are the power behind the porpoise."

G. "The _____ has won the pup and her mother."

H. "The second member of his harem swam toward him, for the birth of a puppy _____ the spring courtship of the porpoise."

I. "Into this silence came the scratch of tiny feet as sand crabs moved over the oyster bed picking up smaller animals that had _____ against the rough shells."

J. "The worm could see vaguely, for it had cups of red seeing _____ at the end of its head."

3. Productive Thinking with the Books of Daniel Manus Pinkwater

The picture books and junior novels of Daniel Pinkwater are perfect examples of the axiom that "the real world is finite and thus limited, but the world of the imagination is infinite and knows no limits."

Reaction to the books of this talented author/artist range from "offbeat" to "genius" and few readers can predict where Pinkwater's imagination will take them next.

Here are examples of productive thinking in action as the author creates a 266-pound tame chicken, a just-filled tooth that receives radio programs, a twelve-year-old multi-billionaire, a band of lizards playing music and a host of other original characters and situations.

The style of the illustrations, described by the artist as "early five-year-old," is exactly right for the fantasy worlds he creates.

THE BIG ORANGE SPLOT. Hastings House, c. 1977. 30 p.

Mr. Plumbean lived on a street where all the houses were the same--"nice." When a seagull drops a can of orange paint on his house, Mr. Plumbean gets an idea that affects the whole neighborhood.

Questions and Activities:

1. No one knows why the seagull was carrying a can of paint, or why he dropped the can. Write a short story giving your explanation for this strange conduct.
(Originality, Elaboration)

2. Which street do you like best? The street at the beginning of the book or the street at the end of the book? Would you like to have a house like the one Mr. Plumbean dreams up? (Decision-making, Evaluation)

3. Find out about housing and building laws in your community. Could you really have a house like Mr. Plumbean's? (Analysis)

4. Design your own dream house. Remember ... "My house is me and I am it. My house is where I like to be and it looks like all my dreams."
(Originality, Elaboration)

BLUE MOOSE. Dodd, Mead, c. 1975. 47 p.

Mr. Breton has a little restaurant on the edge of the big woods. Every day is the same until a talking blue moose comes to stay and serves as head waiter.

Questions and Activities:

1. Think of a first name for the blue moose.
(Originality)

2. Draw a menu for Mr. Breton's restaurant. List all the dishes served. (Elaboration)

3. Make a Blue Moose cook book. Tell how to make all the foods listed on the menu of Mr. Breton's restaurant.
(Fluency, Elaboration)

4. Have a Blue Moose Party
- Sit in a circle and build a fantastic compliment of the chef using adjectives about good food.
(Fluency, Flexibility)
- Play "Pin-the-owl-on-Dave's hat," a version of pin-the-tail-on-the-donkey. (Originality)
- Create a skit based on a scene from the book.
(Originality)
- Give everyone gingerbread, wrapped in string to take home.

5. Write a postcard to the Blue Moose from Mr. Breton. (Originality, Elaboration)

FAT MEN FROM SPACE. Dodd, Mead, c. 1977. 57 p.

When William Pedwee comes home from the dentist, he discovers that his just-filled tooth receives radio programs! While experimenting with his radio tooth, William hears conversations among alien spaceships planning an invasion of Earth. Thousands of fat spacemen float down to Earth, create world-wide panic and gobble up all the junk food they can find.

Activities and Questions:

1. Check it out: can a filled cavity in a tooth really act as a radio receiver? Do some research in the library to find out. (Analysis)

2. Write to a major fast food restaurant chain headquarters. Find out nutritional information about the food they serve. (Analysis)

3. Why is "junk food" called junk food? What is a calorie? Do some research. Create a collage using magazine pictures of junk food. Create a collage of the type of foods you are supposed to eat. (Analysis, Originality)

4. Write a short story in which you meet a creature from space or create a short comic book about spacemen.
(Originality, Elaboration)

THE HOBOKEN CHICKEN EMERGENCY. Prentice-Hall, c. 1977. 83 p.

Arthur Bobowicz brings home a 266-pound tame chicken named Henrietta (instead of a Thanksgiving turkey). Henrietta becomes the family pet, until she runs away and the citizens of Hoboken panic.

Creative Activities:

1. What does your family like to eat on Thanksgiving? Plan a completely new menu for a Thanksgiving dinner. Use a cook book and your imagination! (Originality, Elaboration)

2. Professor Mazzocchi is proud of his strange animals. Invent an unusual animal.
Describe your animal.
Draw a picture of it, or use bits of pictures of real animals from magazines to make a picture of it.
How could your animal be useful to mankind?
(Originality, Elaboration)

3. This book is a satire of the typical story of a boy and his pet. Find four quotes showing satire. (Description)

4. Describe how you would act if you met a 266-pound chicken on the street. (Originality, Elaboration)

5. Draw a map of Hoboken as described in the book. (Use your imagination.) Mark the most important adventures of Arthur and Henrietta. (Originality)
Use your map to create a game. Include the major characters and show the basic plot. Make a game board and activity cards. (Flexibility, Originality)

6. Design a chicken trap to catch Henrietta. Explain

how your trap could catch a 266-pound chicken.
(Problem solving, Analysis, Originality)

THE LAST GURU. Dodd, Mead, c. 1978. 127 p. (Junior
Novel)

Twelve-year-old Harold Blatz has a fantastic ability
to make money. With the help of his Uncle Roy, he quietly
becomes a multi-billionaire.
Then people find out about the boy genius and Harold
becomes a fugitive from publicity. In his search for privacy,
Harold goes to a village high in the mountains of India. There
the monks of the Silly Hat sect discover that Harold is the
reincarnation of their founder.

Questions and Activities:

1. Read and find out further information on religious
sects in the U.S. and the uses of meditation. (Analysis)

2. Discuss satire, elements of, as used in this book.
(Analysis)

3. Is Harold a hero? List the trait you think a hero
should have. Then discover if Harold has any of these traits.
(Evaluation)

LIZARD MUSIC. Dodd, Mead, c. 1976. 157 p. (Junior
Novel)

Victor is left alone when his parents go away for two
weeks and his older sister takes off on a vacation of her own.
While staying up late watching television, Victor is startled
to see a band of lizards playing music. In his search for
answers, he meets the Chicken Man, a man of many names
and activities who often has a chicken in his hat. Together
they visit an invisible island and meet the lizards.

Questions and Activities:

1. Discuss the difference between science fiction and
fantasy. Into which category would you place this book?
(Evaluation)

2. Imagine that you are on your own for the next two weeks. What would you do? List all the activities you would do, the people you would meet, etc. (Fluency, Flexibility)

3. Draw a map and show all the places and people Victor meets in his search for the lizards. (Originality)

4. Create a comic book based on one of the scenes from the book. (Originality, Elaboration)

5. What kind of music would a lizard make? Make up a short composition. Use piano, recorder, or any instrument you can play or invent an instrument to play your composition. (Originality)

6. Write a song for lizards to sing about their island and city. (Originality)

Note: Because this book is so far out and because it deals with a boy on his own, looking out for himself, it is very good for bibliotherapy--ideal for the boy who considers himself "above" books, too cool for his age, too knowing, very bright, but sometimes a non-reader. If you can get this kind of child to just read a book, activities are secondary.

WINGMAN. Dodd, Mead, c. 1975. 63 p.

Donald Chen hated school. He was the only Chinese kid there and nothing good ever happened. Instead of going to school, Donald liked to climb the George Washington Bridge and sit eight stories high on a steel girder. It was there that he first met Wingman, a Chinese super hero like those in Donald's favorite comic books. Wingman opens up a whole new world for Donald.

Questions and Activities:

1. What is Donald Chen's Chinese name? Notice the similarity with the name of Donald's super hero? (Analysis)

2. Why were comic books so important to Donald? (Analysis)

3. Do you have a favorite place to go and get away from people? What fantastic place can you think of that might

be a good get-away-from-it-all place.   Draw a picture of
yourself there.   (Originality)

   4.   Donald was the only Chinese in his school.   What
kind of problems did he have?   (Analysis)

   5.   List each character in this book.   Next to the
name of each person use a noun, a verb, and two adjectives
to describe the person's importance to the play, relation with
the main character, and personality.   (Fluency, Flexibility)

   6.   Develop a super hero of your own and draw a
comic book based on the adventures of your character.
                                    (Originality, Elaboration)

   7.   How do you know that Wingman is a "super hero?"
What is a super hero?   (Analysis)

4.   Critical Thinking and the Books of Jean Merrill

   Jean Merrill has often described herself as a "com-
bative pacifist."   She is a master at creating an unusual
problem or conflict and drawing the young reader along toward
its solution.

   Many of her books are ideal for problem solving or
forecasting (cause and effect) activities which challenge the
reader to go beyond the literal interpretation of the text.   A
favorite theme, the misuse of power, is found in many of her
picture books as well as her junior novels.

   Students who discover the books of Jean Merrill at an
early age will be able to grow with them and to explore her
themes on ever deepening levels.

BOXES.   E. M. Hale & Company, Eau Claire, Wisconsin,
   1953.   Illustrated by Ronni Solvert.

   The Zorn brothers had been making boxes in their
factory for thirty-three years.   These brothers manufactured
all sizes and shapes of boxes for every imaginable product.
   One day the businessmen in the city where the Zorn

brothers lived and worked decided to hold a business convention. The Zorn brothers decided it would be a nice idea to attend this convention and to be able to discuss business matters of all sorts. They were anxious to tell others about the cardboard-box business. Businessmen from all over town wandered around the Royal Banana Leaf Hotel giving away samples of their products and asking interesting questions of other people at the convention.

Much to the disappointment of the Zorn Brothers, people were not the least interested in the making of boxes, only the things that went in them. Sadly, the brothers returned to their factory, and for seven and a half weeks they just sat beside the stove.

Stores and customers began to complain because they couldn't sell or ship anything without boxes. The Mayor of the city declared an emergency, held a special dinner and invited the Zorn Brothers. The most important businessmen in the city were there, all toasting the Zorn Brothers and asking interesting questions about the cardboard-box business. After the dinner party, the brothers returned to the factory to again make cardboard boxes. Soon business in the city was back to normal.

Discussion:

1. Name as many items as you can which are necessary to modern life but which we take for granted. (Fluency)

2. Suppose all zippers, buttons, safety and straight pins disappeared from the world. What would be the result?
(Forecasting)
What could you substitute for these? (Problem solving)

3. Name things in your room at home that came in boxes.
(Fluency)

4. If you had been at the business convention with the Zorn Brothers what business would you like to be in? What questions would you have asked the Zorn Brothers about making boxes?
(Fluency)

5. Write to a box company and find out how boxes are made. Are all made in the same way? Is a box for a McDonald hamburger made of the same material as a cereal box? Can all or some boxes be recycled? (Analysis)

Creative Ideas

Design a box:

1. to ship a kangaroo from Australia to Japan
    (Planning, Problem solving)

2. for a magician to use in a disappearing act
    (Planning, Problem solving)

3. which will fool a friend as to its contents.
    (Problem solving)

THE BUMPER STICKER BOOK. Albert Whitman, 1973.

This is an easy-to-read book which will lure beginning readers by using repetition and high interest. It is a collection of amusing bumper stickers on a variety of cars, trucks and other vehicles. Each page follows the same pattern in the written text so that the beginning reader will be able to master the reading text without difficulty.

Discussion

1. Why do you think people like to put bumper stickers on their cars? Where else have you seen slogans and funny sayings? (Fluency)

2. Which one of the cars or trucks would you like to be riding in? Why? (Evaluation)

Creative Activities

1. Look for bumper stickers on cars. Write down ones you see. Bring them to class. Make a poster or bulletin board display of all the ones the class brings in.
    (Elaboration)

2. Make your own bumper sticker. Try to say something that is especially meaningful to you. (Originality)

3. Sometimes people make banners or buttons. Start a collection of buttons with slogans. Make a banner out of felt or burlap to hang in your room. (Originality)

4. Make up a slogan for the class to use as our class motto. (Originality)

5. Make your own book using a pattern similar to the one in the book. You might like to use the idea of a circus parade. Your pattern might be like this:

Here comes an elephant with a big sign on it and the big sign says TRUNKS FOR SALE

Here comes a _____ with a big sign on it and the big sign says _____ (Elaboration)

EMILY EMERSON'S MOON. Little Brown, 1960.

A father promises his little girl the moon. Her brother says it can't be done. Children will enjoy Father's suggestions to Emily as to how she can have the moon. The story is told in rhyme. The warm, humorous relationship between Emily and her father leaves the reader with a satisfied feeling.

Discussion

1. Would you have been satisfied with Father's solution to the problem? Why or why not? (Evaluation)

2. Father exaggerated when he promised Emily the moon. What are some other examples of exaggeration? (Fluency)

3. How do you think Emily would have felt if Father could not have thought of a way to keep his promise? (Forecasting)

4. Can you think of any other way Father could get the moon for Emily? (Fluency)

Creative Activities

1. Read Many Moons by James Thurber to the class. Compare and contrast the two stories. (Analysis)

2. Father gave Emily a ribbon of six colors which he called a rainbow. He gave her a sunflower for the sun. Let children draw pictures of other things on earth which we could substitute for things in the sky. (Fluency, Flexibility)

3. Prepare a ditto with sentences such as:
You couldn't give someone a river but you could give them a _____ .
You couldn't give someone a mountain but you could give them a _____ .
You couldn't give someone a cloud but you could give them a _____ .
You couldn't give someone a star but you could give them a _____ .
You couldn't give someone lightning but you could give them _____ .
(Originality)

HERE I COME, READY OR NOT, by Jean Merrill and Frances Gruse Scott. Albert Whitman, 1970.

This is another "hiding" book by Merrill and Scott. This time two children are hiding in a large country barn. The pictures and text take the young reader into many nooks and crannies in a barn where they can see the animals, farm workers doing their jobs and many farm tools and implements.

Discussion

1. Big farms sometimes have a bell hanging outside. What do you think is the purpose of the bell?
(Fluency, Flexibility)

2. The barn in the story is a very big place. The children look very small when they are hiding. How do you think they felt when they were hiding way up in the hayloft or among the cows? Would they have felt differently if they lived in the city and were visiting than they might have felt if the farm was their home? (Forecasting)

3. Why do you think the children were READY for lunch? What are some things you have done that have given you a good appetite? (Fluency)

4. Make a list of all of the animals shown in the book. See if you can find out something interesting about

each one. Find out why a farm would have each animal shown. Make a chart like the one below:

Name of Animal	Something about the animal	Why it is needed

(Research)

5. There are many tools and implements shown in this book. See if you can find out what some of them are used for. Draw pictures of several that interest you. Write one or two sentences to go with each tool. Display the pictures on the bulletin board. Give the display a title. (Research)

6. The book shows the workers sorting apples. Find out more about apples. Use the encyclopedia or a science book. Cut an apple in half. Now cut another apple the same way. Do you see some patterns? How are they different when you cut in different directions? (Visual Literacy)

7. There is a big barrel marked cider near the apples. What does cider have to do with apples? How is cider made? Can you trace a glass of cider from seed to the drink? Make a picture report showing the steps from seed to cider. (Research)

HIGH, WIDE AND HANDSOME. Young Scott Books, 1964.

This Burmese version of an old folk tale uses the device of a story within a story. It is the tale of a city slicker, Rolling Stone, and three country rascals, High, Wide and Handsome, who have a story-telling contest to see who can tell a story so astonishing that it will not be believed. Each animal sets out to tell the tallest tale he can, but the city slicker is not tricked and in the end he tricks the three with his tall tale.

Discussion

1. Sometimes people or animals are given names because of their characteristics. Why do you think each animal was given his name? Can you think of other names for these four animals? Which names best suited the character?
(Fluency, Flexibility)

2. Do you think the three animals learned a lesson

from their experience? Do you think they will try to take
advantage of a stranger again?   (Forecasting)

Creative Activities

    1.   Pretend to be either High, Wide or Handsome.
Make up a different story to tell to Rolling Stone. Remember it must be so astonishing that he could not possibly believe it. Now pretend to be Rolling Stone and see if you can
create a new ending. Maybe you will want Rolling Stone to
lose the game. How would your story be different then?
                        (Originality, Elaboration)

    2.   Using the same four characters: a monkey, a pig,
a fox and a dog, make a stick puppet for each. Change the
setting for the story. You could make it happen here in our
town or in another part of the country. Make a background
that would show where the story now takes place. Dress your
stick puppets as they would be for the new setting. Put on a
puppet play. Groups of three or four could work together.
         (Forecasting, Originality, Elaboration)

HOW MANY KIDS ARE HIDING ON MY BLOCK? by Jean
    Merrill and Frances Gruse Scott. Albert Whitman, 1970.

    A group of children playing hide and go seek in an
urban area are hiding in various places along a city block--a
candy store, TV repair shop, second-hand store and many
other locations are shown. The youngest finds the cleverest
place of all to hide. The story has very little plot but young
children will enjoy trying to guess where children are hiding
and will become intrigued by the many details of the shops
shown in the pictures.

Discussion

    1.   The children in a city neighborhood had a good
time playing together. Tell about some of the games you
play with children in your neighborhood. What kind of behavior makes for a fun time with others? What makes a
game not much fun?   (Fluency)

    2.   The picture in the front of the book shows eleven
children. The story says that ten children are hiding. Can

you explain why there are eleven children in the picture?
(Analysis)

3. Where would you hide if you were playing with these children? Pretend that you are playing this game in your own neighborhood. How is your neighborhood different? Where would you hide in your neighborhood? Pretend that you are in a shopping center. Where would you hide?
(Decision-making)

Creative Activities

1. Have children cut out pictures of stores and other places from magazines. Paste these on a large piece of paper and make a mural. The class can then make a hiding story using their own mural. (Elaboration)

2. Make a list of all of the different kinds of work that are shown in the book. Children can choose one of the occupations to tell about or write a simple report using information books from the library. (Research)

MARIA'S HOUSE. Atheneum, 1975.

Maria thinks that art should be beautiful. She attends an art class at the museum. Her art teacher has asked her to draw a picture of her own house, but Maria's house is an ugly, run-down apartment building. Maria can draw a beautiful house in the suburbs and her teacher will never know the difference. But Maria's mother will know and Mama says that art must be true. Children will see Maria's struggle to make her decision and understand what it really means to be an artist.

Discussion

1. What did Mama mean when she said, "Art must be true?" Can you think of some "art" that you have seen that has not been true? Mama also said that for an artist, everything turns to pictures. Can you think of some everyday things that you see that turn to pictures?
(Visual Communication, Analysis)

2. What qualities can you name that describe Mama?

Miss Lindstrom? Maria? Which of these characters is the most interesting? Why do you think as you do? (Evaluation)

3. What can you see in an art museum? Tell about a time you have been to an art museum. What other kinds of museums are there? (Fluency)

Creative Activities

1. Draw a picture of your own house. Let others know about the feelings of the people who live there by the things you put in the picture. (Visual Communication)

2. For Maria, knowing that Saturday was coming made the rest of the week wonderful too. Write a short paragraph telling about the kind of Saturday you would be looking forward to. (Originality, Elaboration)

THE PUSHCART WAR. William R. Scott, 1964. (Junior Novel)

The Pushcart War is a story set about ten years in the future. It tells of a war in New York City between the trucks and the pushcarts. It started when a Mighty Mammoth truck ran down a pushcart belonging to Morris the Florist, and it grew in intensity into a full-scale battle. It is a satire on many aspects of modern-day life including politicians, war, big business, the news media, fads and marches. The central theme seems to be however, that corruption can still be overcome by the "little man" working with other "little men," and that ordinary citizens can have an impact on the modern world's problems. The satire seems to become more timely as the years go by.

Discussion

1. Big trucks on the highway today are causing many problems. What do you think should be done about it? Should bigger trucks be allowed? Should trucks be banned from highways? (Problem solving)

2. What other problems can you find in the story that parallel the problems of today? Can you think of any problems in your school that would be similar to the pushcart peddlers' problems? (Analysis)

3.   What qualities did the pushcart peddlers have that helped them work together to win the war?   What book characters do you know that have overcome an enemy that was bigger and more powerful?   (Fluency, Flexibility)

4.   Can you recall any events in The Pushcart War that would have a parallel in the American Revolution?
(Analysis)

5.   Analyze Mayor Cudd's Peanut Butter speech for propaganda techniques.   (Analysis)

6.   Frank the Flower became a fad across the country.   What fads are currently popular?   How did they get started?   (Fluency)

Activities

1.   Think of something that irritates or bothers you. Now think of something you are in favor of.   Fill in the phrase: The _____ against the _____. Make up a situation where a war between the two sides would be started.   How did it start?   What happened next?   How was the war finally won?   (Originality, Elaboration)

2.   Have a TV panel show.   Decide on a moderator and four "experts."   Give names and qualifications to your experts.   Discuss the two sides of the war you wrote about or choose a real subject such as "Big trucks on the highway."
(Analysis)

3.   Write a letter to the editor about a current problem that you feel is important and really send it.   Suggest a solution to the problem.   (Problem solving)

4.   Suppose that Harry-the-Hot Dog had been the peddler who became famous instead of Frank-the-Flower.   Pretend that you are the president of his fan club.   What would you have used for a symbol of your club?   Think up a password and a motto or pledge.   (Originality, Elaboration)

PLEASE DON'T EAT MY CABIN.   Albert Whitman, 1971.

Adam had a special gift.   He could tame and make friends with almost any animal.   His mother and his grand-

mother, Tessie, were proud of his ability and encouraged him
until one summer when Adam went to stay with Tessie in her
cabin in the woods.   Adam had plans for all the animals he
would tame to keep Tessie company.   She was pleased with
the woodchuck, the mole, the mouse and the owl, but she refused to have anything to do with the motherless porcupine because she was afraid it would eat the wooden posts of her
cabin, as is the natural habit of porcupines.   The problem
is solved when Adam and Tessie learn why porcupines do this
and what to do about it.   Children will enjoy learning about
Adam's methods as they read about the way he works with
animals.

Discussion

1.   At Tessie's camp everyone did just as they pleased.
What were some of the unusual things Adam and Tessie did?
What would you do if you could do just as you pleased?   Should
everyone be able to do as they please all the time?   Why was
it possible for Tessie to let Adam do as he pleased?
                                        (Forecasting, Analysis)

2.   The neighbor shot the mother porcupine because it
was destroying things.   Was this a good reason to kill the
animal?   What else could he have done?   How do you decide
whether or not to kill something like a porcupine?
                                        (Evaluation)

Creative Activities

Write an article about porcupines using the information
in the story.   Add other information which is plausible but
not factual.   Entitle your article "Facts and Fiction About
Porcupines."   Challenge your friends to separate your facts
from your fiction.   (Elaboration, Analysis)

SHAN'S LUCKY KNIFE.   E. M. Hale & Company, Eau Claire,
   Wisconsin, 1970.   Illustrated by Ronni Solbert.   (Junior
   Novel)

Shan lived in the hills of Burma and once a week he
would come down to the village in Bhamo to the bazaar.   He
enjoyed listening to the traders tell of their world-wide travels.
When Shan came to Bhamo he would always bring with him his

two favorite possessions, a shoulder bag and a kan (a musical instrument), and would refuse offers of trade or money for these two favorite possessions. One day, a clever and greedy trader named Ko Tin came to Bhamo looking for boatmen. His tricks and cheating ways were well known to the traders. Shan was hired to do a man's work at half the usual pay. During the trip to Rangoon, Ko Tin did indeed trick Shan into selling him his favorite shoulder bag and kan for money to buy a cock. On the return journey Shan fed the cock rice and was charged all of his wages by Ko Tin to pay for the rice. Once back in Bhamo, when Shan realized he had been tricked, he sold the cock and bought two identical knives from a trader. A second time he was hired by Ko Tin as a boatman. Shan showed only one of the knives to the other boatmen while keeping the second one hidden. Shan claimed it to be a lucky knife. One afternoon Ko Tin noticed Shan sharpening his knife beside the boat. Ko Tin yelled at Shan for neglecting his work. Shan was startled and the knife fell into the river. He borrowed a knife and made a mark on the side of the boat. Shan remarked that it was a lucky knife and that he would retrieve it after supper.

Having seen this as an impossible task Ko Tin bet Shan his boat and all the possessions on it for Shan's wages that Shan would be unable to find his knife. Shan dove into the water, removing the second knife which was hidden in his belt. He returned to the surface with the knife. Shan wisely took over the boat, and was able to get back his kan and his shoulder bag. The traders of Bhamo still tell the story of the lucky knife.

Discussion

1. Why do you think Shan's shoulder bag and musical instrument were so important to him? (Analysis)

2. Shan had two favorite possessions. If you were going to work on the river as a boatman like Shan, what two favorite possessions of yours would you take? What would make them important to you? (Evaluation)

3. Has anyone ever cheated you out of anything? When? How did you feel? What did you do then? Do you think Shan's way of tricking Ko Tin was fair? (Evaluation)

4. Using just the pictures in the book, in what ways

are the homes different from yours? Why are they on stilts?
What things would you like about living there? What things
would you tell a friend from Burma about where you live?

(Analysis)

Creative Ideas

Write your own tale like Shan's. Change some char-
acters: Shan would be _____; Ko Tin would be
_____; Burma would be _____. Instead
of becoming a boatman you might work _____;
The han could be _____; The Kan could be
_____; The two knives could be _____.

(Elaboration)

THE SUPERLATIVE HORSE. William R. Scott, 1961.
(Junior Novel)

The Superlative Horse was suggested by a Taoist tale
in a book written around 350 B.C. It tells of Duke Mu in
Ancient China, whose greatest interest was his stable of
20,000 blooded horses. He loved his chief groom, Po Lo,
as a brother and respected his judgment and ability. Po Lo
was getting old and it was time to find someone to take his
place. The Duke was astonished when Po Lo suggested a
young boy, Han Kan, the son of a fuel hawker. Duke Mu
trusted Po Lo enough to go along with the suggestion and
agreed to give Han Kan a chance, provided he could pass the
test of choosing a horse fit for the Duke's stable. In spite
of the predictions of the jealous Chief Minister, Han Kan
proves Po Lo's judgment to be sound and finds a superlative
horse.
The appeal of the book is in the gentle tone that leaves
the reader with a very satisfied feeling.

Discussion

1. Duke Mu was a powerful ruler. What qualities
did he have that showed that he was a good ruler? What kind
of person was Wang Ho, the Chief Minister?   (Analysis)

2. How would the Duke's kingdom have been different
if he had listened to Wang Ho? Do you think Wang Ho got

what he deserved at the end of the story?

(Forecasting, Evaluation)

Creative Activities

1. Look up the word <u>superlative</u> in the dictionary. Write two or three sentences about something that you think is superlative. Use a thesaurus to find synonyms for superlative. Try to use the word superlative in your conversation within the next 24 hours. Can you think of a slang word which might come from superlative?

2. Write a commercial or design an advertisement for something you really feel is superlative. Stress both value and price in your ad. Be sure you understand the difference. (Analysis, Planning, Originality)

THE TOOTHPASTE MILLIONAIRE. Houghton Mifflin, 1972. (Junior Novel)

When Rufus Mayflower became upset over the price of a tube of toothpaste (79¢), he bet he could make a gallon for that amount. This led to Rufus and his friend Kate going into the business of manufacturing and selling toothpaste for 3¢ a tube, with 1¢ profit. The story follows the toothpaste enterprise from its beginnings in Rufus' kitchen through establishing a corporation, issuing stocks, getting a bank loan, employing workers and advertising, until Rufus' early retirement at age 13.

The story gives children an understanding of some of the problems of the business world and shows how our economic system works.

Discussion

1. Do you think that a twelve-year-old could actually set up a business and make a million dollars? Can you think of any product that an ordinary person could make at much less cost than it is sold for in the store? (Analysis)

2. Rufus and Kate both had qualities that were needed in their successful business. What qualities and skills did Rufus contribute? Kate? If you had been one of the children in Rufus' neighborhood, in what way could you have contributed

to the business?   What skills or abilities do you have that
would be useful in some kind of business?

(Analysis, Forecasting)

Creative Activities

1.   Many grocery stores now have plain label (no
brand name) products.   Make a list of products and prices
of some of these items.   Compare these with brand name
items.   Find out how much money can be saved by buying
plain label products.   How much money could be saved in a
year?   Is there a difference in quality?   (Analysis)

2.   Make your own toothpaste.   Put your favorite
flavoring in it.   Think of a name for your toothpaste and design a box for it.   (Planning, Originality)

3.   In Chapter Nineteen Kate wrote a movie script but
didn't get to finish it.   What ending could you add to Kate's
script?   (Elaboration)

THE TRAVELS OF MARCO.   Alfred Knopf, 1956.

Marco, an adventurous city pigeon, visits many people
and places in New York City, looking for food he likes.   Marco
finds that he does not like much of the food that his new
friends offer him, but he does like the people.   The reader
meets a variety of ethnic groups and gets a glimpse of New
York City life.

Discussion

1.   Marco found that different people eat different
kinds of food.   In what other ways are people you know different from one another.   (Fluency)

2.   Tell about some kind of food that you have eaten
that you felt was different.   Did you like it?   What or why
not?   (Evaluation)

3.   Marco could see in four directions from his rooftop.   Pretend that you are on the roof of your school or another tall building.   What would you see in each direction?

(Forecasting)

Activities

     1. The sign that Marco saw said FORWARD. Design a sign or billboard that would cause someone to want to do something new.   (Planning, Originality)

     2. See if you can find out what ethnic group each of the foods Marco ate came from. Look up the food words in the dictionary. There are hints in the pictures in the book too. Match the food with the ethnic group.   (Research)

spaghetti	d	a.	Chinese
rice	a	b.	Jewish
bagel	b	c.	Southern U. S. A.
olives	e	d.	Italian
melon	c	e.	Greek
gugelhupf	f	f.	German

     Name as many cities, states or countries as you can that begin with the letters below.   (Fluency)

F rance	M _____
O _____	A _____
R _____	R _____
W _____	C _____
A _____	O _____
R _____	
D _____	

     Now find a food and a describing word for each of the letters.   (Fluency)

F ried	frankfurters	M ashed	melons
O _____	_____	A _____	_____
R _____	_____	R _____	_____

W _____   _____   C_____   _____

A _____   _____   O_____   _____

R _____   _____

D _____   _____

APPENDIX

A SELECTED BIBLIOGRAPHY FOR
GIFTED AND TALENTED STUDENTS AND THEIR TEACHERS

Allison, Linda. The Reason for Seasons: The Great Cosmic Megagalactic Trip Without Moving from Your Chair. Boston: Little, Brown and Company. $4.95

Anderson, Carolyn. Brain Stretchers (Book 2). Troy, MI: Midwest Publications.

Antell, Gerson and Walter Harris. Economics for Everybody. New York: Amsco School Publications.

Armstrong, Louise. How to Turn Lemons in Money: A Child's Guide to Economics. New York: Harcourt Brace Jovanovich, 1976. $1.75

Arneson, D. J. Mork and Mindy Code Puzzles from Ork. New York: Cinnamon House (Grosset and Dunlap Co.), 1979. 95¢

Ballard, Jim. Stories With Holes. Amherst, MA: Mandala Publishing Co. $2.50

Barr, Stephen. Puzzlequiz: Wit Twisters, Brain Teasers, Riddles, Puzzles and Tough Questions. New York: Thomas Y. Crowell Co., 1978. $8.95

Bererter and Anderson. Thinking Games. Toronto: The Ontario Institute for Studies in Education, 1975. (Book 1: Ages 5-9; Book 2: Ages 9 and older)

Biggs, Edith and James R. MacLean. Freedom to Learn. Menlo Park, CA: Addison-Wesley Publishers. $6.36 (Math)

Biondi, Angelo. The Creative Process. Buffalo, NY: DOK Publishers, Inc., 1972.

Blake, Jim and Barbara Ernst. The Great Perpetual Learning Machine. Boston: Little, Brown and Company, 1976. $12.95

Breyfogle, Ethel, et al. Creating a Learning Environment: A Learning Center Handbook. Santa Monica, CA: Goodyear Publishing Company, Inc., 1976.

Brown, A.E. and H.A. Jeffcott, Jr. Absolutely Mad Inventions. New York: Dover Publications.

Buckeye, Donald. Experiments in Probability and Statistics. Troy, MI: Midwest Publications. $1.50

Burns, Marilyn. The Book of Think. Boston: Little, Brown and Company. $4.95

Burns, Marilyn. Good For Me: All About Food in 32 Bites. Boston: Little, Brown and Company. $4.95

Burns, Marilyn. The I Hate Mathematics Book. Boston: Little, Brown and Company. $4.95

Burns, Marilyn. I Am Not a Short Adult. Boston: Little, Brown and Company. $4.95

Burns, Marilyn. This Book Is About Time. Boston: Little, Brown and Company. $4.95

Cardozo, Peter and Ted Menten. The Whole Kids Catalog. New York: Bantam Books. $5.95

Carle, Eric. I See a Song. New York: Thomas Y. Crowell Company, 1973. $4.50

Casteel, J. Doyle. Learning to Think and Choose: Decision-Making Episodes for the Middle Grades. Santa Monica, CA: Goodyear Publishing Company, Inc., 1978. $8.95

Castle, Sue. Face Talk, Hand Talk, Body Talk. Garden City, NY: Doubleday and Company, Inc., 1977.

Catalogue of Curriculum Resources. Science Teachers' Association of Ontario, Donco Quality Printers, 212 Division St., Kingston, Ontario K7K321, Canada.

Cavin, Tony. The Bright Red Porcupine. Harlin Quist Publishers, Inc., 1969. $2.95

Charlip, Remy. Arm in Arm. New York: Parents Magazine Press.

Clark, Barbara. Growing Up Gifted. Columbus, OH: Charles E. Merrill Publishing Co., 1979. $16.95

Cobb, Vicki. Science Experiments You Can Eat. Philadelphia: J. B. Lippincott Company. $1.95

Debnam, Betty. The Best of the Mini Page. Kansas City: Sheed Andrews and McMeel, Inc. (Subsidiary of Universal Press Syndicate), 1977. $6.95

Decker, Isabelle. 100 Novel Ways with Book Reports. New York: Scholastic Books.

Deindorfer, Scott. (Age 10) Dear Scott. New York: Workman Publishing, 1978. $3.95

deKay, Ormonde, Jr. Rimes de la Mère Oie. (Mother Goose rhymes rendered into French) Boston: Little, Brown and Company, 1971. $7.50

Delacorte, Peter and Michael Witte. The Book of Terns. New York: Penguin Books, 1978. $3.95

DeMille, Richard. Put Your Mother on the Ceiling: Children's Imagination Games. New York: Viking Press.

Devi, S. Figuring: The Joy of Numbers. New York: Harper and Row Publishing Company, 1977. $6.95

DeVito, Alfred and Gerald H. Krockover. Creative Sciencing: A Practical Approach. Boston: Little, Brown and Company, 1976.

Do It to It Workbook, for Teachers of Gifted and Talented. Gifted Child Project, ESEA Title IV-C, Leon County Public Schools, 2757 W. Pensacola St., Tallahassee, FLA 32304. 904-487-1520 (Handbook for Teachers $2.44, game is $2.90, and workbook is $2.70), 1978.

Edmund Scientific Company, 55 Edscorp Building, Barrington, New Jersey 08007, 609-547-3488 (For scientific supplies and equipment)

Ephron, Delia. How to Eat Like a Child. New York: The Viking Press, 1978. $7.95

Fern, Leif. Geocabulary Cards. San Diego CA: Kabyn Publications. $8.40

Fern, Leif. The Teacher and 52 Ways to Have Fun with My Mind. (Teacher Guide) San Diego, CA: Kabyn Books, 1976. 70¢

Fern, Leif. Teaching for Thinking: 311 Ways to Cause Creative Behavior. San Diego CA: Kabyn Books. $7.25

Fern, Leif. The Thinking Kabyn. San Diego, CA: Kabyn Publications. $8.00

Fern, Leif. Writing Kabyn: Sentences and Paragraphs, Products, Technology, Assessment and Editing. San Diego, CA: Kabyn Publications. (Full set $105.00)

Fern, Leif and Ursula Golesz-Benson. 42 Ways to Have Fun with My Mind, 52 Ways to Have Fun with My Mind, 62 Ways to Have Fun with My Mind, and 72 Ways to Have Fun with My Mind. San Diego, CA: Kabyn Books, 1976. $2.50

Fixx, James F. Games for the Super Intelligent and More Games for the Super Intelligent. New York: Doubleday and Company, Inc., 1976.

Fixx, James F. Solve It. Garden City, NY: Doubleday and Company, Inc., 1978.

Fluegelman, Andrew. The New Games Book. Garden City, NY: Dolphin Books (Doubleday and Co.), 1976. $4.95

Frank, Marjorie. If You're Trying to Teach Kids How to Write, You've Gotta Have This Book! Nashville, TN: Incentive Publications, Inc., 1979.

Gardner, Martin. Perplexing Puzzles and Tantalizing Teasers. New York: Simon and Schuster (Children's Book Division), 1969.

Gardner, Martin. Space Puzzles: Curious Questions and Answers About the Solar System. New York: Simon and Schuster. $4.95

German, Joan. Brain Boosters Activity Cards. Palos Verdes Peninsula, CA: Frank Schaffer Publications, Inc., 1974.

Golick, Margie. Deal Me In. New York: Jeffrey Norton Publishers.

Gordon, William J. J. and Tony Poze. Strange and Familiar Series. (Books I, II, III). Cambridge, MA: SES Associates, 1975. (Order from The Analogy, 4040 University, Suite B, Des Moines, Iowa 50311

Gwynne, Fred. A Chocolate Moose for Dinner. New York: Windmill Paperbacks, 1976. $2.95

Gwynne, Fred. The King Who Rained. New York: Windmill Paperbacks, 1970. $1.95

Harnadek, Anita. Basic Thinking Skills Series (workbook). Troy, MI: Midwest Publications, Inc., 1977.

Harnadek, Anita. Classroom Quickies. Troy, MI: Midwest Publications, 1979. $2.95 for book, $9.95 for duplicating masters.

Harnadek, Anita. Critical Thinking Book One (workbook and teachers' edition). Troy, MI: Midwest Publications, Inc., 1978.

Harnadek, Anita. Deductive Thinking Skills Series (workbooks). Troy, MI: Midwest Publications, Inc., 1978.

Heller, Ruth. The Complete Optical Riddle Book: Opt-iddles. New York: Golden Press, 1977. $1.95

Hickman, Norman. The Quintessential Quiz Book: Little-known Oddities of Fact and Fiction. New York: St. Martin's Press. $8.95

Higgins, James. Tongue Twisters. Boston: Houghton Mifflin Company, 1973.

Holt, Michael and Ronald Ridout. The Big Book of Puzzles. New York: Alfred A. Knopf, 1972. $2.50

Hubert, Karen M. Teaching and Writing Popular Fiction: Horror, Adventure, Mystery, and Romance. New York: Virgil Books. $4.00

Human Individual Potentialities, Unicornucopia: A Guidebook for Gifted and Talented. Tempe: Kyrene School District

#28, 8700 South Kyrene Road, Tempe, Arizona 85284, 1977.

Hutchinson, Helene D. Mixed Bag: Artifacts from the Contemporary Culture. Glenview, IL: Scott, Foresman and Company, 1970.

Junior Planetarium for $15.00. Steven Manufacturing Co., 224 East Fourth Street, Hermann, Missouri 65041

Kanigner, Herbert. Everyday Enrichment for Gifted Children at Home and School. Los Angeles, CA: National/State Leadership Training Institute on the Gifted and Talented, Civic Center Tower Building, Suite PH-C, 316 West Second St., Los Angeles, CA 90012, 1977.

Kaplan, Sandra and Sheila Madsen. Think-Ins, An Approach to Relevant Curriculum, Stressing Creative Thinking and Problem Solving. Monterey Park, CA: Creative Teaching Press, 1974. $6.95

Katzman, Carol and Joyce King. Economy Size. Santa Monica, CA: Goodyear Publishing Co. Inc., 1978.

Keller, Charles. Ballpoint Bananas and Other Jokes for Kids. Englewood Cliffs, NJ: Prentice-Hall, Inc.

Kirst, Werner and Ulrich Diedmeter. Creativity Training: Becoming Creative in 30 Minutes a Day. New York: Peter H. Wyden, Inc., 1971.

Laliberte, Norman and Richey Kehl. 100 Ways to Have Fun With An Alligator and 100 Involving Art Projects. Blauvelt, NY: The Art Education Publishing Company, Inc. 10913

Landis, Melodee. The Class Menagerie: A Compilation of Exciting Activities for Secondary School Students. (Federal Project #600-7604827, Office of Gifted and Talented) Lincoln, NE: Nebraska State Dept. of Ed. (301 Centennial Mall South, Lincoln, Nebraska 68509) June, 1978.

Latta, Richard. Games for Travel. Los Angeles, CA: Price/Stern/Sloan Publishers, Inc., 1976. $1.25

Lawless, Ruth. Programs for Gifted/Talented/Creative

Children (For Little or No Money). Buffalo, NY: DOK Publishers, 1977.

Lederman, Janet. Anger and the Rocking Chair: Gestalt Awareness with Children. New York: Viking Press.

LeSieg, Theo. Would You Rather Be a Bullfrog? New York: Random House, Inc., 1975. $2.95

Lewis, M. B. Mork and Mindy Puzzles. Cinnamon House (Grosset and Dunlap Co.), 1979. 95¢

Lewis, Richard, ed. Miracles. New York: Simon and Schuster, 1966.

Lipman, Matthew. Ethical Inquiry: An Instructional Manual to Accompany Lisa. Upper Montclair, NJ: IAPC, Montclair State College, 1979.

Lipman, Matthew. Harry Stottlemeier's Discovery. Upper Montclair, NJ: Institute for the Advancement of Philosophy for Children, Montclair State College, 1977.

Lipman, Matthew. Lisa. Upper Montclair, NJ: IAPC, Montclair State College, 1976.

Lipman, Matthew. Philosophical Inquiry: An Instructional Manual to Accompany Harry Stottlemeier's Discovery. Upper Montclair, NJ: IAPC, Montclair State College, 1979.

Lipman, Matthew. Suki. Upper Montclair, NJ: IAPC, Montclair State College, 1978.

Lipman, Matthew and Ann Margaret Sharp. Growing Up With Philosophy. Philadelphia: Temple University Press, 1978. $20.00

Lipson, Greta B. and Baxter Morrison. Fact, Fantasy and Folklore: Expanding Language Arts and Critical Thinking Skills. Carthage, IL: Good Apple, Inc., 1977.

Lobel, Arnold. Frog and Toad Together. New York: Harper and Row, Inc., 1972. $4.95

Ludewijh, T. et al. The Way Things Work: An Illustrated Encyclopedia of Technology. 2 vols. and Special Edition for Young People. New York: Simon and Schuster.

Lyon, Harold C. Learning to Feel--Feeling to Learn. Columbus, OH: Charles E. Merrill Publishing, Co.

Making It Strange Series (workbooks #1-4 and a teacher's manual). Harper and Row, Publishers, Inc., 1968.

Manchester, Richard B. The Mammoth Book of Word Games. New York: Hart Publishing Company, Inc. 1976. $6.95

Marcy, Steve and Janis Marcy. Mathimagination (several workbooks). Palo Alto, CA: Creative Publications, Inc., 1973.

Martel, Jane. Smashed Potatoes. Boston: Houghton Mifflin Co., 1974. $2.95

Meyer, Jerome. Arithmetricks: Amazing and Bewildering Stunts and Tricks with Numbers. New York: Scholastic Books, 1965.

Miklowitz, Gloria D. and Peter Desberg. Ghastly Ghostly Riddles. New York: Scholastic Book Services, 1977. 95¢

Minnesota Environmental Science Foundation, Sampling Button Populations, Genetics Variation, Transect Studies. (Order from The National Wildlife Federation, Educational Service, 1412 16th St. NW, Washington, D.C. 20036

Mira, Julio. Mathematical Teasers. New York: Barnes and Noble Books (Harper and Row), 1970.

Moffett, James. Interaction. Boston: Houghton Mifflin Co.

Mohan, Madan and Virginia Risko. Perception Stimulators. Buffalo, NY: Disseminators of Knowledge (DOK) Publishers, Inc.

Mosler, Gerard. The Puzzle School. New York: Abelard-Schuman, 1977.

Myers, R.E. and E. Paul Torrance. Invitations to Speaking and Writing Creatively. Boston, MA: Ginn and Company.

Nash, Bruce and Greg Nash. Pundles. New York: The Stonesong Press (Grosset and Dunlap, Inc.), 1979. $2.50

Neukirchen, Mary Beatrice. Classroom Activities for Literature and Reading. Buffalo, NY: DOK Publishers, Inc. 1973. (grades 1-6) $2.25

Noller, Ruth B. and Sidney Parnes, and Angelo M. Biondi. Creative Actionbook. (Actionbook and Guide). New York: Charles Scribner's Sons, 1976.

Parnes, Sidney. AHA! Insights into Creative Behavior. Buffalo, NY: The Creative Education Foundation, Inc., 1975. $1.50

Parnes, Sidney. Creative Behavior Guidebook. New York: Charles Scribner's Sons, 1967.

Parnes, Sidney J. Creativity: Unlocking Human Potential. Buffalo, NY: DOK Publishers, Inc., 1972.

Pape, Donna Lugg and Jeannette Grote. Puzzle Panic. New York: Scholastic Book Services, 1976. 95¢

Penrose, Gordon. Dr. Zed's Zany Brilliant Book of Science Experiments. Woodbury, NY: Barron's Educational Series, Inc., or in Canada: Grecy de Pancier Publ., 1977. 59 Front St. East, Toronto, Ontario, Canada.

Polette, Nancy. Activities with Folktales and Fairytales. O'Fallon, MO: Book Lures, Inc., 1979.

Polette, Nancy. Book Encounters of the Best Kind. O'Fallon, MO: Book Lures, Inc., 1979.

Polette, Nancy. Having Fun with Books by Robert Kraus. O'Fallon, MO: Book Lures, Inc., 1979.

Polette, Nancy. Library Skills Thru Folk Music. O'Fallon, MO: Book Lures, Inc., P.O. Box 9450, 63366, 1979.

Polette, Nancy. Pick a Pattern for Creative Writing. O'Fallon, MO: Book Lures, Inc., 1979.

Price, Roger. Droodles #2. Los Angeles: Price/Stern/Sloan Publishers, Inc., 1974. (410 North La Cienega Blvd., Los Angeles, CA: 90048. $1.25

Price, Roger. The World's Worst Riddles. Los Angeles: Price/Stern/Sloan Publishers, Inc., 1974. $1.25

Probability Kit. Creative Teaching Associates, P.O. Box 293, Fresno, CA 93708. $6.95

The Productive Thinking Program: A Course in Learning to Think. Columbus, OH: Charles E. Merrill Publishing Co. (set of 15 workbooks, teacher's guide, and spirit masters--Middle school and Junior High).

Quinn, Vernon. Fifty Card Games for Children. Cincinnati: U.S. Playing Card Co. $1.00

Raboff, Ernest. Marc Chagall: Art for Children. (One artist of a series.) Garden City, NY: Doubleday, 1968.

Raudsepp, Eugene and George P. Hough. Creative Growth Games. New York: Jove Publications, Inc. (Harcourt Brace Jovanovich), 1978. $3.95

Reasoner, Charles R. For Kids Only. New York: Delacorte Press, 1977. $4.95

Resources for Decision Making. 1978 Catalog of the Psychological Corporation, 4640 Harry Hines Blvd., Dallas, TX 75235.

Reed, W. Maxwell. Patterns in the Sky: The Story of the Constellations. New York: William Morrow. $4.75.

Renzulli, Joseph. The Enrichment Triad Model: A Guide for Developing Defensible Programs for the Gifted and Talented. Mansfield Center, CT: Creative Learning Press, Inc., 1977.

Renzulli, Joseph. New Directions in Creativity. (Mark A, Mark I, Mark 2, Mark 3) New York: Harper and Row, 1976.

Rice, Ruth. Solve It If You Can! New York: Scholastic Book Services, 1974.

Sackson, Sid. Beyond Words. New York: Random House, Inc., 1977. $2.95

Samson, Richard W. Thinking Skills: A Guide to Logic and Comprehension. Stamford, CT: Innovative Sciences, Inc., 1975. $6.95

Sandburg, Don. The Legal Guide to Mother Goose. Los Angeles: Price/Stern/Sloan Publishers, Inc., 1978. $2.50

Sarnoff, Jane and Reynold Ruffins. The Code and Cipher Book. New York: Charles Scribner's Sons, 1975.

Saterstrom, Mary. Educators Guide to Free Science Materials. Randolph, WI: Educators Progress Service. $10.25

Schaffer, Frank. Secret Codes for Fun. Palos Verdes Peninsula, CA: Frank Schaffer Publishers, 1973.

Schlicter, Carol. TAP (Talents Unlimited Program). Mobile, Alabama: Board of School Commissioners of Mobile Co. P. O. Box 1327 36601

Schneider, Tom. Everybody's a Winner: A Kid's Guide to New Sports and Fitness. Boston: Little, Brown and Company $4.95

Schwartz, Alvin. Kickle Snifters and Other Fearsome Critters. New York: J. B. Lippincott Co. (A Bantam Skylark Book), 1976. $1.25

Schwartz, Alvin. A Twister of Twists: A Tangler of Tongues. New York: J. B. Lippincott Co. (A Bantam Skylark Book), 1972. $1.75

Seuling, Barbara. The Last Cow on the White House Lawn and Other Little Known Facts About the Presidency. New York: Doubleday and Co. Inc., 1978.

Seuling, Barbara. The Teeny Tiny Woman. Cedar Grove, NJ: Roe Publishing, Inc., 1976. (Puffin Books, 1978)

Seymour, Dale, et al. Aftermath (workbooks). Palo Alto, CA: Creative Publications, 1971.

Shepley, Joseph, T. Playing with Words. Englewood Cliffs, NJ: Prentice-Hall, Inc., 1960.

Silverstein, Shel. Where the Sidewalk Ends. New York: Harper and Row, 1974. $8.95

Sparke, William and Clark McKowen. Montage: Investigations in Language. New York: The Macmillan Co.

Stanford, Gene and Barbara Dodds Stanford. Learning Discussion Skills Through Games. New York: Citation Press (Scholastic Magazines), 1969.

Stanish, Bob. Sunflowering: Thinking, Feeling, Doing Activities for Creative Expression. Carthage, IL: Good Apple, Inc., 1977.

Stone, Harris, A. The Chemistry of a Lemon and The Chemistry of Soap. Englewood Cliffs, NJ: Prentice-Hall.

Stone, Harris, S. and Bertram Siegel. Have a Ball. Englewood Cliffs, NJ: Prentice-Hall. (Science)

Striker, Susan and Edward Kimmel. The Anti-Coloring Book. New York: Holt, Rinehart, and Winston, 1978. $3.95

Suid, Roberta Koch and Murray Suid. Proverbs. Boston: Houghton Mifflin Co., 1973.

Tangrams: 330 Puzzles. Dover Publications. $1.50

Teachers from the Dallas ISD. AAAH's: Many Mini-Courses for the Academically Talented Student. Dallas, TX: Dallas Independent School District, 1977. (grades 4-8)
Up Periscope: Research Activities for the Academically Talented Student (grades 4-8)
To Teach for Thinking: Mini-courses for Academically Talented Students. (grades 4-8)

Thornley, Wilson. Short Story Writing. New York: Bantam Books, Inc. $1.25

Torrance, E. Paul. Torrance Tests of Creative Thinking, Directions Manual. Lexington, MA: Personnel Press, 1966.

Wasserman, Irving. Rebuses. Boston: Houghton Mifflin Co., 1973.

Weitzman, David. My Backyard History Book. Boston: Little, Brown and Company, 1975. $4.95

Williams, Frank. A Total Creativity Program for Individualizing and Humanizing the Learning Process. Englewood Cliffs, NJ: Educational Technology Publications, 1972.

Williams, Margery. The Velveteen Rabbit. New York: Doubleday and Company, Inc., 1971. $3.95

World's Largest Maze #1. Los Angeles: Price/Stern/Sloan
    Publishers, Inc., 410 North La Cienega Blvd., Los
    Angeles, CA 90048. $1.00

Worthy, Morgan. AHA! A Puzzle Approach to Creative
    Thinking. Chicago: Nelson-Hall Inc., 1975.

Wurman, Richard Sarl, ed. Yellow Pages of Learning Re-
    sources. Cambridge, MA: The MIT Press. $5.95

Young, Sharon. Mathematics in Children's Books: An Annota-
    ted Bibliography Preschool Through Grade 3. Creative
    Publications, 1979.

Zephyros Staff. Imagination. San Francisco: Zephyros
    Educational Exchange.

Magazines and Publications

The Council for Exceptional Children. 1920 Association Dr.,
    Reston, Virginia 22091.

Creative Education Foundation, Inc. State University College
    at Buffalo, Chase Hall, 1300 Elmwood Ave., Buffalo,
    New York 14222. (Creative Problem Solving Institute).

Games. P.O. Box 10145, Des Moines, Iowa 50340.

G/C/T (Gifted, Creative, Talented). Box 66654, Mobile,
    Ala., 36606. (5 times a year, $15.00 a year).

The Gifted Child Quarterly. National Association for Gifted
    Children 217 Gregory Dr., Hot Springs, Ark. 71901
    (Membership $20.00, includes journal free).

Thinking, The Journal of Philosophy for Children. Institute
    for the Advance of Philosophy for Children, Montclair
    State College, Upper Montclair, New Jersey 07043.

Professional Reading on the Gifted Child

Arieti, S. Creativity: The Magic Synthesis. New York:
    Basic Books, 1976.

Biondi, A. & Parnes, S. Assessing Creative Growth. Great
    Neck, NY: Creative Snyergetic Association, 1976.

Clark, Barbara, Growing Up Gifted. Columbus, OH: Charles
    E. Merrill, 1979.

Colangelo, Nicholas and Zaffrann, Ronald T. New Voices in
    Counseling the Gifted. Dubuque, IA: Kendall/Hunt
    Publishing Co. , 1979.

Feldhusen, John F. and Treffinger, Donald. Creative Thinking
    and Problem Solving in Gifted Education. Dubuque, IA:
    Kendall/Hunt Publishing Co. , 1980.

Gallagher, James J. Teaching the Gifted Child. Boston,
    MA: Allyn and Bacon, Inc. , 1975.

Gowan, John; Khatena, Joe; and Torrance, Paul, eds. Edu-
    cating the Ablest. 2d ed. Itasca, IL: Peacock, 1979.

Guilford, J. Pa. Way Beyond the IQ. Buffalo, NY: Creative
    Education Foundation, 1977.

Keating, D. P. Intellectual Talent: Research & Development.
    Baltimore, MD: Johns Hopkins University Press, 1976.

Khatena, Joe. The Creatively Gifted Child. New York:
    Vantage Press, Inc. , 1978.

MacKinnon, Donald W. In Search of Human Effectiveness.
    Buffalo, NY: Creative Education Foundation, 1978.

Meeker, Mary N. The Structure of Intellect: Its Interpretation and Uses. New York: Charles E. Merrill Publishers, 1969.

Newland, Ernest T. The Gifted in Socio-Educational Perspective. Englewood Cliffs, NJ: Prentice-Hall, Inc., 1976.

Osborn, Alex. Applied Imagination. New York: Charles Scribner's Sons, 1963.

Parnes, Sidney E. Creative Behavior Guidebook. New York: Charles Scribner's Sons, 1967.

Parnes, Sidney; Noller, Ruth; and Biondi, Angelo. Creative Actionbook. New York: Charles Scribner's Sons, 1976.

Renzulli, J. The Enrichment Triad Model. Mansfield Center, CT: Creative Learning Press, Inc., 1977.

Renzulli, J., and Barbe, W. B. Psychology and Education of the Gifted. 2d ed. New York: Halsted Press, 1975.

Rothenberg, Albert and Hausman, Carl. The Creativity Question. Durham, NC: Duke University Press, 1976.

Seagoe, May V. Terman and the Gifted. Los Altos, CA: William Kaufmann, Inc., 1975.

Stanley, Julian; George, William; and Solano, Cecelia. The Gifted and the Creative: A Fifty-year Perspective. Baltimore, MD: The Johns Hopkins University Press, 1977.

Torrance, E. P. Dimensions of Early Learning: Creativity. San Rafael, CA: Dimensions Publishers, 1969.

Torrance, E. P. Encourage Creativity in the Classroom. Vol. 8 of Issues and Innovations in Education Series, edited by J. C. Bentley. 8 vol. Dubuque, IA: William C. Brown Company, 1970.

Torrance, E. P. The Search for Satori & Creativity. Buffalo, NY: The Creative Education Foundation.

Torrance, E. P. and Myers, R. E. Creative Learning and Teaching. New York: Dodd, Mead, and Company, 1970.

Whitmore, Joanne Rand. Giftedness, Conflict and Under-
    achievement. Boston, MA: Allyn and Bacon, Inc.,
    1980.

Williams, Frank. A Total Creativity Program for Individual-
    izing and Humanizing the Learning Process. Vol. 1,
    "Identifying and Measuring Creative Potential"; Vol. 2,
    "Encouraging Creative Potential." Englewood Cliffs,
    NJ: Educational Technology Publishers, 1972.

RESOURCES FOR TEACHERS AND PARENTS

National Association for Gifted Children   (NAGC)

Executive Office
2070 County Road H
St. Paul, Minnesota
(612)784-3475

Business Office
217 Gregory Drive
Hot Springs, Arkansas
71901
(501)767-6933

Joyce Juntune
Executive Director

Publishes: The Gifted Child Quarterly
A membership newsletter

Membership - $26.00 a year
Additional publications available

Office for Gifted and Talented (OGT)
U.S. Department of Education
6th and D Streets, S.W.
Washington, D.C. 20202
(202)245-2482   Toll Free - (800)245-2482

Lyon Harold
Director

Administers grants to states and local districts

Council for Exceptional Children (CEC)
The Association for the Gifted (TAG)
1920 Association Drive
Reston, Virginia 22091
(800)336-3728

Dr. Frances Karnes
TAG President
Center for Gifted Studies
University of Southern Mississippi
Hattiesburg, Mississippi 39401

Publishes: Exceptional Children
Journal for the Education of the Gifted
TAG Update - Membership newsletter

Membership - $35.00-$40.00 a year depending on the
state you live in
Additional publications available

American Association for Gifted Children (AAGC)
15 Gramercy Park
New York, New York 10003
(212)473-4266

Marjorie Craig,
Executive Director

Publications available.

National State Leadership Training Institute on the Gifted and
the Talented (N/S - LTI-G/T)
316 West Second Street, Suite PH-C
Los Angeles, California 90012
(213)489-7470

Irving S. Sato
Director

Publishes: Monthly bulletin

Subscription - $15.00 a year
Additional publications available

National Association for Creative Children and Adults (NACCA)
8080 Springvalley Drive
Cincinnati, Ohio 45236
(513)631-1777

Ann F. Isaacs, Consultant

Publishes: The Creative Child and Adult Quarterly
             It's Happening - Newsletter

Membership - $20.00 a year
Additional publications available

Northeast Exchange Educational Improvement Center (NE-EIC)
    New Jersey Department of Education
    207 Delsea Drive
    RD 4, Box 209
    Sewell, New Jersey   08080
    (609)228-6000

Contact - Theodore J. Gourley

Publications available

Study of Mathematically Precocious Youth (SMPY)
    Department of Psychology
    127 Ames Hall
    The Johns Hopkins University
    Baltimore, Maryland   21218
    (301)338-7087

Julian Stanley, Director

Publications available

INDEX